The Long Marriage

ALSO BY MAXINE KUMIN

MAXINE AND VICTOR KUMIN WITH GUS AND CLAUDE (1978). *Kelly Wise*

MAXINE KUMIN

The Long Marriage

POEMS

W. W. NORTON & COMPANY

NEW YORK LONDON

For information about permission to reproduce selections from this book,
write to Permissions, W. W. Norton & Company, Inc., 500 Fifth Avenue,
New York, NY 10110

The text of this book is composed in Bembo with the display set in Centaur
Composition by Tom Ernst
Manufacturing by the Maple-Vail Book Manufacturing Group
Book design by Chris Welch
Production manager: Julia Druskin

Library of Congress Cataloging-in-Publication Data

Kumin, Maxine, date.
The long marriage : poems / Maxine Kumin.
p.   cm.
ISBN 0-393-04351-7
I. Title.

PS3521.U638 L63 2001

811'.54—dc21   2001034553

W. W. Norton & Company, Inc., 500 Fifth Avenue, New York, N.Y. 10110
www.wwnorton.com

W. W. Norton & Company Ltd., Castle House,
75/76 Wells Street, London W1T 3QT

1 2 3 4 5 6 7 8 9 0

For Victor, "on the dark lake . . ."

Contents

VI

VII

I

Skinnydipping with William Wordsworth

I lie by the pond *in utter nakedness*
thinking of you, Will, your epiphanies
of woodcock, raven, rills, and craggy steeps,
the solace that seductive nature bore,
and how in my late teens I came to you
with other Radcliffe *pagans suckled in*
a creed outworn, declaiming whole swatches
of "Intimations" to each other.

Moist-eyed with reverence, lying about
the common room, rising to recite
Great God! I'd rather be . . . How else
redeem the first flush of experience?
How else create it again and again? *Not in*
entire forgetfulness I raise up my boyfriend,
a Harvard man who could outquote me
in his Groton elocutionary style.

Groping to unhook my bra he swore
poetry could change the world for the better.
The War was on. Was I to let him die
unfulfilled? Soon afterward we parted.
Years later, he a decorated vet,

I a part-time professor, signed the same
guest book in the Lake District. Stunned
by coincidence we gingerly shared a room.

Ah, Will, high summer now; how many more
of these? *Fair seed-time had my soul,*
you sang; what seed-times still to come?
How I mistrust them, cheaters that will flame,
gutter and go out, like the scarlet tanager
who lights in the apple tree but will not stay.

Here at the pond, your *meadow, grove, and stream*
lodged in my head as tight as lily buds,
sun slants through translucent minnows, dragonflies
in paintbox colors couple in midair.
The fickle tanager flies over the tasseled field.
I lay my "Prelude" down under the willow.
My old gnarled body prepares to swim
to the other side.
                                  Come with me, Will.
Let us cross over sleek as otters,
each of us bobbing in the old-fashioned breaststroke,
each of us centered in our beloved Vales.

Thinking of Gorki While Clearing a Trail

It wasn't exactly raining but
a little wetness still dribbled down.
I had been reading and sorrowing
and set out with the dogs as an antidote.
They went ahead snuffling in the leaf plaster.
Despite the steady snick of my clippers
boletus mushrooms kept popping soundlessly
out of the ground. How else account for
the ones with mouse-bites out of the caps
when I doubled back on my tracks?

The animals have different enzymes
from us. They can eat amanitas
we die of. The woodpeckers' fledglings
clack like a rattle of drumsticks each time
crumpled dragonflies arrive and are thrust
into the bud vases of their gullets.
The chipmunk crosses in front of me
tail held up like a banner. Who knows
what he has in his cheeks? Beechnuts
would be good, or a morsel of amanita.

Gorki disliked his face with its high
Mongol cheekbones. *It would be good to be*

a bandit, he said, *to rob rich misers*
and give their money to the poor. Saturnine
Gorki, at the 1929 International Congress
of Atheists. By then he was famous, but
twice, in his teens, he tried to kill
himself. Called before an ecclesiastical
tribunal and excommunicated, he declared
God is the name of my desire.

The animals have no Holy Synod to
answer to. They simply pursue their vocations.
In general, I desire to see God lifting
the needy up out of their dung heap,
as it is written. I did not seek this
ancient porcupine curled in the hollow
of a dead ash tree, delicately encoded
on top of a mountain of his own dung,
pale buff-colored pellets that must have
taken several seasons to accumulate.

At this moment, I desire the dogs, oblivious
so far, not to catch sight or scent of him.
I am the rightful master of my soul
Gorki said, and is this not true of the porcupine?
Born Aleksei Maksimovich Peshkov
he chose his own name—*gorki*—bitter
and a century later I carry him
like a pocket guide on this secret trail
clearing and wool-gathering as we go.

Imagining Marianne Moore
in the Butterfly Garden

Surrounded, blundered into by
these gorgeous tropical ephemerae,
we watch their pinwheel colors compose
an arcane calligraphy on air
under a quarter-acre of fine mesh.

I almost step on a slender young botanist
in a shocking-pink smock, lying flat
to pollinate certain recalcitrant flowers
with a single-haired paintbrush.
You bend to inspect her handiwork
your twice-wound braids frizzing red against
the sun to form a sort of web.

Marianne, I was appalled you dared
to chloroform a cat and then
dissect it at Bryn Mawr. Was it
the miniaturist impulse even then,
a schoolgirl's red desire
to see fine things in place?

When our guide uses her second and third
fingers to clasp a palm-sized Heliconid
by one wing, you murmur approvingly,

Precisionist. We peer at the owl eye it wears
as a scare tactic. I see a frisson pierce you
just as the peacocks on the grass at Oxford
once made your hair stand on end, the eyes
of their tail feathers holding you fast.

Worlds apart we are undergraduates
again. Letting the brilliant mimicry
shiver through us.
We are the beasts, you whisper
and I nod, releasing you.
The noiseless Heliconid
soars to another silent flower.

The Greenhouse Effect

Again, look overhead
How air is azurèd. . . .
—THE WORKS OF GERARD MANLEY HOPKINS

The paper in this book was
produced from pure wood pulp without
the use of chlorine or any other
substance harmful to the environment.

I bore it to the indifferent cashier
who could not know that according
to Robert Bridges' introduction
although touchy and arrogant, you
had great sweetness, nor how sweet
it is to replace my lost edition
loaned to a student forty years ago
with this paperback wearing your portrait
as a rosy-lipped boy on the cover.

Dear Gerard, how gentle, how British
the rest of the disclaimer, which ends:
thereby conserving fossil fuels and
contributing little to the greenhouse effect.

Flesh and fleece, fur and feather,
Grass and greenworld all together. . . .
In your lifetime and most of mine, greenhouse
suggested roses out of season,

fleshy gladiolas, even European
cucumbers trained to trellises:

in short, the kind of fervor
that made you burn those early poems for
the love of God, you would have said,
on becoming a Jesuit. For the love
of posterity Bridges saved
most of them, and for the love
of the environment, Wordsworth Editions
reprinted you <u>with ah! bright wings</u>.

Mother of Everyone

MURIEL RUKEYSER 1913–1980

Once a day I lie flat on my back
stretch out the bent sapling of my torso
and raise my four-pound yellow dumbbell.
Working out makes me think of Muriel.
Muriel after her next-to-last stroke
standing a little spraddle-legged for balance
the way I do, although I try to hide
my disequilibrium
by leaning casually against
railings, blackboards, doorjambs.

Passionate Muriel, tough as a tree trunk,
her sure voice containing a vibrato—
had it always been there? I felt it
as a splinter she worked past, line by line
declaiming *surely it is time for the true grace of women* . . .
a young and fervent Muriel evacuated
from Barcelona at the outbreak
of the Spanish civil war on an overcrowded boat
chartered by Belgians when consulates were helpless . . .
obdurate Muriel demanding human rights
for Kim Chi Ha in his Korean cage
a poet in solitary, *glare-lit, I hear,*
without books, without pen or paper

Muriel eulogizing Matty—*Defend us*
from doing what he had to do. . . .
Harvard's F. O. Mattheissen
my favorite professor, who leapt from the closet
out of a Boston hotel window—
and I thought how she was the first woman-poet
I knew who was willing to say the unsaid.

In rehab I was learning how to put one foot
in front of the other, how to lift
a teaspoon from the soup bowl to my lips.
Three months of that. I had
a one-pound weight. They strapped it to my wrist.

In "Resurrection of the Right Side" Muriel tells it:
Word by stammer, walk stammered, the lurching deck of earth.
Who but Muriel, picking her way back
through the earthquake that flattened her, learning
all over again how to smooth a stagger, hold a pen,
enunciate the language she coaxed from her mouth,
who but she could build poems from such rubble.
Muriel, mother of everyone.

Rilke Revisited

Carrying a single
long-stemmed iris
you walk through Prague,
dressed entirely in black,
an uncooked bard whose work,
according to Lou Andreas
Salome, is *florid,*
romantic and obscure.

She makes you change
your name (René at birth),
revise your crabbed longhand,
and put your infantilized
white feet on wet grass.
You work at a stand-up desk
to force the sluggish blood
down to your numb appendages.

You become a vegetarian,
you breakfast on
imported Quaker Oats.
And then come lovers, fans,
translators, your name

on the tongues of literati.
Your angels somersault,
then hover in midair.

I feel them pass by
causing the tips of my hair
to rise crackling
from the sidewise
swipe of their wings.

Pantoum, with Swan

FOR CAROLYN KIZER

Bits of his down under my fingernails
a gob of his spit behind one ear
and a nasty welt where the nib of his beak
bit down as he came. It was our first date.

A gob of his spit behind one ear,
his wings still fanning. I should have known better,
I should have bitten him off on our first date.
And yet for some reason I didn't press charges;

I wiped off the wet. I should have known better.
They gave me the morning-after pill
and shook their heads when I wouldn't press charges.
The yolk that was meant to hatch as Helen

failed to congeal, thanks to the morning-after pill
and dropped harmlessly into the toilet
so that nothing became of the lost yolk, Helen,
Troy, wooden horse, forestalled in one swallow

flushed harmlessly away down the toilet.
The swan had by then stuffed Euripedes, Sophocles
—leaving out Helen, Troy, Agamemnon—
the whole house of Atreus, the rest of Greek tragedy,

. . .

stuffed in my head, every strophe of Sophocles.
His knowledge forced on me, yet Bird kept the power.
What was I to do with ancient Greek history
lodged in my cortex to no avail?

I had his knowledge, I had no power
the year I taught Yeats in a classroom so pale
that a mist enshrouded the ancient religions
and bits of his down flew from under my fingernails.

II

Hard Frost: On a Line by Hopkins

No need now for the newspaper mulch
topped with spoiled hay. It will become
by summer one friable creation.

Irrelevant now the owl balloons at four corners
and the spray made from pulverized seeds
of the neem, revered shade tree of Asia.

The bean plants have fallen to skeletons.
The forgotten tomatoes have imploded
and a black melt has seized the squash vines

but all of the root crops linger, serene in their cubbyholes.
Beets, carrots, parsnips, the tapered white cones known as daikon.
Potatoes still threaded to one another in their labyrinth.

As the Pequots planted fish in their corn hills
I shovel a dead mouse mottled with maggots
hidden how long in a riot of rhubarb leaves

deep down under a barefaced sunflower
deep down for dearest freshness.

Why There Will Always Be Thistle

Sheep will not eat it
nor horses nor cattle
unless they are starving.
Unchecked, it will sprawl over
pasture and meadow
choking the sweet grass
defeating the clover
until you are driven
to take arms against it
but if unthinking
you grasp it barehanded
you will need tweezers
to pick out the stickers.

Outlawed in most Northern
states of the Union
still it jumps borders.
Its taproot runs deeper
than underground rivers
and once it's been severed
by breadknife or shovel
—two popular methods
employed by the desperate—
the bits that remain will

spring up like dragons' teeth
a field full of soldiers
their spines at the ready.

Bright little bursts of
chrome yellow explode from
the thistle in autumn
when goldfinches gorge on
the seeds of its flower.
The ones left uneaten
dry up and pop open
and parachutes carry
their procreant power
to disparate venues
in each hemisphere
which is why there will always
be thistle next year.

The Politics of Bindweed

I have lived all season among the bindweed.
I have spied on their silent Anschluss,
the bugles of their flowers, the dark guy wires
they put down into earth from which to fling
slim vines that burgeon into airy traps.

At eye level I have seen them strangle aster,
milkweed, buttercup; I have taken note of
their seemingly random entanglement by tendril
of the whole drowsy meadow. My own ankles
have been tugged at and held fast by these fanatics.

These barbarian cousins of morning glory
mean to smother the clover, drive out the livestock,
send scouts to infiltrate the next hayfield,
exploit the ties of family and class
until they rule from hedgerow to hedgerow.

Wherefore all season on my hands and knees
I have ripped out roots, stems, ringlets and blossoms.
I have pursued every innocent threadlike structure
to its source, then plucked it. My chosen task is
to reestablish the republic of grasses.

The Brown Mountain

What dies out of us and our creatures,
out of our fields and gardens,
comes slowly back to improve us:
the entire mat of nasturtiums
after frost has blackened them,
sunflower heads the birds
have picked clean, the still
sticky stalks of milkweed
torn from the pasture, coffee grounds,
egg shells, moldy potatoes,
the tough little trees that once
were crowded with brussels sprouts,
tomatoes cat-faced or bitten into
by inquisitive chipmunks,
gargantuan cucumbers gone soft
from repose. Not the corn stalks and shucks,
not windfall apples. These
are sanctified by the horses.
The lettuces are revised
as rabbit pellets, holy with nitrogen.
Whatever fodder is offered the sheep
comes back to us as raisins
of useful dung.

· · ·

Compost is our future.
The turgid brown mountain
steams, releasing
the devil's own methane vapor,
cooking our castoffs so that from
our spatterings and embarrassments—
cat vomit, macerated mice,
rotten squash, burst berries,
a mare's placenta, failed melons,
dog hair, hoof parings—arises
a rapture of blackest humus.
Dirt to top-dress, dig in. Dirt fit
for the gardens of commoner and king.

The Potato Sermon

Exhumed at the end of the season
from their caverns of love, their loamy
collectives, the little red Norlands
here nibbled at, there split or malformed
turn up in blind budded clusters
smooth-cheeked, delicate, sometimes
surrounding a massive progenitor
while the thick-skinned long-keeping
Kennebecs that at first pretend
to be tree roots or fossils or wrist bones
are rewards for the provident.

You must do this on your knees
switch hitting, with long pauses
closing your eyes as you tunnel
the better to focus on feeling.
The dirt that packs under your fingernails
forms ten grin lines as if you had clawed
through bricks of bitter chocolate.
It's an Easter egg hunt underground.

Once mounded up in the larder
there is starch for the orphan's belly
there is radiant heat for the hungry.

Go forth as if to partake in
night failing, day beginning.
Go forth. The task is simple.
Deliver the warty earth apple.

The Exchange

The neophyte animal psychic
visits my barn at midday.
She is wearing for the occasion
aquamarine eyeliner
a sequined bow in her hair
and a slippery nylon jacket
my gelding loves to explore
with his delicate muzzle.

What do the horses, those thousand-pound
engines of passion and flight,
the horses, long my conspirators,
tell her, who's newly beguiled?
She says the old broodmare knows
how in the other life
I dined abroad with crows
carrion my caviar.

She says the sloe-eyed fillies
know in the next I am meant
no more to eat flesh but simply
to pick grass, switch flies, and roll
as my horses roll after work
thudding down like a wagonload

of watermelons to tip
from side to side on the sand
scratching the struts of their backs.

And yes, I can feel the itch
ascending my spine as we
observe this ritual together
something, she now confesses
she's never witnessed before.
I tell her the ancient Hindus
moved by this scene, inferred
how their gods and demons, while
churning the ocean of milk
in order to make nectar, erred
and out of chaos brought forth
with dished profile, kind eye
and mane woven from many strands of silk
this magnificence, the horse.

Highway Hypothesis

Nothing quite rests the roving eye
like this long view of sloping fields
that rise to a toyshop farmhouse
with matchstick barns and sheds.
A large yellow beetle spits silage
onto an upturned cricket while
several inch-high cars and trucks
flow soundlessly up the spitcurl drive.

Bucophilia, I call it—
nostalgia over a pastoral vista—
where for all I know the farmer
who owns it or rents it just told his
wife he'd kill her if she left him and
she did and he did and now here come
the auctioneer, the serious bidders
and an ant-train of gawking onlookers.

III

.

Calling Out of Grays Point

They call it a hand-hole, this pit
the size of a child's coffin. In it
Purvis, caked with muck, sweats
trying to solve the tangle
of Bell South's wires and grids.
Fierce with prickers, a jungle
of palmettos surrounds him.

Ever since the day she moved in
she's been without a phone.
The instrument sits mute on
her desk (along with a new translation
of *Introduction to Metaphysics*)
awaiting installation.

                    Purvis
hails from the Ozarks, he isn't one
to mince words. *See what*
some fuckup's gone and done?
Blue-white's sposed to be
tied to blue-white right here, see
how this asshole's got it attached
to red-green? About what I'd expect.

                             . . .

Heidegger asked, wherein
is the ground of being?
She wonders, given
today's technology
and his gift for introspection
if Heidegger's query, implying
one must suffer to fit in,
would cover these failed connections.

Purvis returns at dawn.
From his tool belt dangle
pliers, wires, screw drivers, bangles
of linked connectors for the lines
still dead. Mice? Moisture?
Crimps in the cable? Trouble-shooter
Purvis vows by day's close
service will be restored.

From his coffin he blasphemes the Lord
loudly (he hadn't guessed
that wire was hot). At sunset
pudgy, garrulous Purvis—it's
hard not to like him—proffers
the gift of his beeper number
packs up his boom box
climbs in his white truck
and departs for a six-pack
and a shower.

                              .   .   .

Alone, she tries not
to yield to angst
the inherent emptiness
of a life she cannot call out of.
She misses Purvis, the cream cheese
and bagel she gave
him half of, his hourly harangues
at her door to report how close
he is to success.
But another day
goes down to darkness.

Next morning somebody else—
Eric, who's slender and terse.
Eric, who doesn't make small talk.
Purvis's beeper no longer shrills.
Introvert Heidegger pales.
Businesslike Eric unspools
half a mile of wire, loops it over
the fence, along the sill
of the house, under palmetto cover
and in through her screen.
Jury-rigged but never mind.
Presto! A dial tone!
She never sees Purvis again.

Opening the Doors of Perception in Grays Point

Louder than panzers
a dozen jets scream overhead.
The knife edge of solitude
presses against her throat.
Displaced, a paying guest

she slides back the doors
of the bathhouse to let in
the staghorn ferns, the dry
chitter of palm leaves
the black blight on the roses.

Chlorine lilts from the turquoise pool.
She puts her winter self in a chaise longue
under the kind sun. Leisure
is sticky. Thirst troubles her
like an unanswered letter.

Soundlessly at dusk the cats arrive.
Over the rooftop, over the fence's
iron palings, the padlocked gates
to take up their stations in pools of black.
Under a table, behind a flower pot.

                              .   .   .

The cats jitter and box in the dark.
Sleepless she dials and redials
her memory call service.
These must be hers, the calm syllables
that speak her name on command.

All night long planes
crisscross the patio streaking
toward London or Rome.
In time she will learn to sleep
through their raw music.

8 A.M. in Grays Point

At the bloody crossroads of narrative and culture
to quote Matthew Arnold, she goes out for her
morning power walk around the perimeter.
Others are doggedly working out: the smiling
bald man with headphones, two sleek older women
not quite as leathery as she but pumping
their elbows as she does, and glistening
with her sweat. One poor soul stubbing along
on her four-prong aluminum crutch, and a young
dog walker enmeshed in several leashes.

Despite the rush hour traffic at the bloody
crossroads beyond the high stucco wall, she
knows she has entered Paradise.
The people who live here are doctors and lawyers
who carefully space their children
eat from the five food groups, endorse
ballet and theater. Their foreign cars
are waxed and polished. Their lives are guarded
by speed bumps. Sprayed with poisons, their lawns
wear discreet little Danger signs.

At the crossroads the 8 o'clock bus disgorges the maids
languidly moving toward their employment.

They carry string bags, they walk, when they can, in the shade,
in sandals or old shoes with cutouts for bunions.
They are not for the most part Anglo, or thin,
these Marias. Even the young ones look old.
By rote to the voice of the vacuum, the swish of the wet mop
all day they will jiggle and waltz on broad hips
the babies and toddlers who reach up to be held.
Without them, Paradise would teeter and fall.

Afoot in Grays Point

Without a single peep-hole
through the crimson blare
of bougainvillea, she jogs
the empty streets, voyeur

peering down private drives
through iron gates, to keep
secret watch how heavily
the freighted houses sleep

and as the day grows brighter
how cobalt blue the bins
curbside for cardboard, plastic jugs
junk mail, newsprint, and cans

how jauntily Green Meadows
Landscape Care, three palms
a freehand frieze on the panel truck
shatters the sunrise calm.

How Zephyr Hills thereafter
succeeds the mowers' pother
hiking natural spring water from
one shoulder to the other

· · ·

Miami Rescue Mission
following close behind
to suck up a scuttled desk beside
a television gone blind

in which she sees reflected
a bank of cumuli
which shift as she approaches, while
a single dove nearby

tests the newly sheared
and pesticided lawn
then breasts the stuccoed wall that keeps
the golden people in.

My Life

WITH THREE LINES CULLED FROM HENRY VAUGHAN

While my life is taking place
in four rented pink and green rooms
where faux purple grapes adorn a table lamp
at dusk a cruise ship as long as a city block
and seven storeys high outside my window
is nudged to sea by tugboats, trumpets, and fireworks
and on an adjoining pier a cargo container
disgorges twenty dehydrated humans
along with three corpses.

While my life is taking place
a televangelist explains from a drop-down set
in the fluorescent kitchen how heaven
is shaping up to be a seamless silver city filled
with Vaughan's bright *shootes* of everlastingnesse.

I am smashing bright shoots of garlic when
my parents waft past on the highway
the dead travel while my here-and-now fingers
are picking up and putting down knives, vinegar;
while my fingers and forehead are rebraiding
bright shoots, dream wisps arrive from my past
all gone into the world of light! namely, a long line
of waif dogs; the starveling mare I rescued

who never learned to love me but abided
safely and aloof; my three departed die-hard
brothers still estranged; and now the police are called
to round up a dozen straying illegals
who swam ashore from cigarette boats beaching
amid the suntans and volleyball of snowbirds.

O wasteful heaven, the Jewel of the Just!
Placeless heaven full
of disorderly remembrance, come,
come in while my life is taking place.

IV

Ghazal: On the Table

I was taught to smooth the aura at the end,
said my masseuse, hands hovering at the end.

Inches above my placid pummeled self
did I feel something floating at the end?

Or is my naked body merely prone
to ectoplasmic vapors to no end?

Many other arthritics have lain here
seeking to roll pain's boulder end on end.

Herbal oils, a CD playing soft
loon calls, wave laps, bird trills now must end.

I rise and dress, restored to lift and bend,
my ethereal wisp invisible at the end.

Wagons

Their wheelchairs are Conestoga wagons drawn
into the arc of a circle at 2 P.M.

Elsie, Gladys, Hazel, Fanny, Dora
whose names were coinage after the First World War

remember their parents tuned to the Fireside Chats,
remember in school being taught to hate the Japs.

They sit attentive as seals awaiting their fish
as the therapist sings out her cheerful directives:

Square the shoulders, lean back, straighten the knee
and lift! Tighten, lift and hold, Ladies!

They will retrain the side all but lost in a stroke,
the spinal cord mashed but not severed in traffic.

They will learn to adjust to their newly replaced
hips, they will walk on feet of shapely plastic.

This darling child in charge of their destiny
will lead them forward across the prairie.

The Woman Who Moans

is not in pain.
She is making the sounds
of speech. She drums
her heels, a child strapped
against her will
in the stroller. Perhaps
she protests, perhaps
she agrees in full
with the therapists
when they wheel her chair
to the standing table
and fasten her legs
to supports that brace
her upright. See how
she clings to the tabletop?
Whether she begs
or resists release
is hard to tell
from the song she sings,
moans that ascend
to a blackbird's warble.

Eventually,
restrained like a pup

on a leash, she will learn
once again to walk.
One on each side
they will hold her up
by her voyaging belt
but the sounds she emits
will not change. The fault-
line in her brain
will continue to gape
and the bus, the Forty-
second Street bus
that caught her midstep
and hurled her aloft
will go on transporting
the rest of us.

Grady, Who Lost a Leg in Korea, Addresses Me in the Rehab Gym

He fondles the stump.
See these here flaps along the seam?
Dog ears, they're called.
Gotta work em down
like pie dough with a roller pin
get em smooth enough to set against
the fiberglass. It's light as eggshell.
Gwan, try my leg. Pick it up.

Never could wear the one
they fit me to at the V.A.
Mostly metal, weighed a ton
to cart around, but now—
nodding at another amputee
practicing between
the parallel bars—*I'm gonna*
give it another try.

Grady calls me Parrot Head
—the metal cage that holds
my broken neck—I call him Ahab.
Even though we're little more
than fellow inmates in
the neuro unit on the topmost floor

down here we're life companions
makin a game of it.

Now those guys over there
in chairs? They got the sugar.
Diabetes. Works like a cannibal,
one leg, then the other.
Toes first, foot next, then the knee.
And when they got no other way
to stop the rot, they saw
the goddamn leg off up to here.

He draws his hand across his groin.
Can't fit a thing to that.
You gotta have a stump.
They call em double amputees.
You see em outside on good days
doin wheelies, rearin back
to jump the sidewalk curb
like a bunch of acrobats

makin a game of it.
And once I get the hang of this
I'm gonna waltz my way around
the gym. And then
I'm gonna ask you, Parrot Head,
Wanna dance?

Grand Canyon

Past the signs that say *Stop! Go Back!*
We Are Friendly Indians! past the tables
of garnet and red rock, of turquoise and silver,
past horses thin as paper, profiled
against a treeless horizon, I come
to where all roads converge, I stand
at each of a dozen jumping-off places
with my fellow cripples, my fellow Americans
peering into our national abyss.

Outings for wheelchair postulants
are regular affairs here on the brink
of this improbable upheaved landscape;
the clinic for chronic pain my therapists
back East referred me to is,
by Western measurements, just down the road.
The group is quiet. Wind music lobs
endless songs to would-be suicides
from the river bottom's Loreleis,
a redemptive eight-hour hike below us,
but no one's leapt this week. Some travel
both ways on the bony backs of mules,
slaves forever on this tortuous trail.

. . .

Despite the crowds, despite the kitsch,
this mesa, this elevated plain
has always been on my life list.
Life-list, a compound noun in my
directory. The fact is, I'm alive.
The fact is, no conjecture can resolve
why I survived this broken neck
known in the trade as the hangman's fracture,
this punctured lung, eleven broken ribs,
a bruised liver, and more. Enslaved

three months in axial traction, in what they call
a halo, though stooped, I'm up. I'm vertical.
How to define chronic pain?
Maddening, unremitting,
raying out from my spinal cord
like the arms of an octopus, squeezing,
insidious as the tropic anaconda. . . .
The experts are fond of saying
spinal cord injuries are like
snowflakes; no two are ever the same
but while you're lying on the table, unfrocked
—no one tells you this—the twists and pummels,
the stretches and presses are identical.
One size of therapy fits all.

Who practices for disaster? Who
anticipates that the prized horse will bolt,
that you will die/should have/didn't?

That a year will pass before
you can walk the line they ask a drunk to,
or balance on one foot. Who knew
the dumb left hand could be retrained
to cut meat, brush teeth, and yet the day I signed
my name in loose spaghetti loops beneath
the intended line, I wept. We joked
I'd buy a stamp pad, roll my thumb,
some day receive outrageous sums
from Sotheby's for my auctioned print,
brave banter we all but choked
on, but better than the cant that says,
be grateful you're alive, thank God.
Implicit in it, *you've had it too good.*

What would the friendly Indians trade
to break loose from the white man who
reduced them to servitude?
What would the suicidal barter
for deliverance from
the Sisyphean boulder
they daily roll uphill?
What would I trade to regain
my life the way it was?
From pillar to abyss
the answer echoes still:
The word is *everything.*

V

William Remembers the Outbreak of Civil War
1983

I took off my clothes and walked naked. There were
people killing boys just for their clothes.

I walked with the rest of my Dinka clan
a thousand kilometers, single file.

We blistered our feet in the desert dirt
the flyaway dirt of southern Sudan.

If my mother sat down beside me today
I wouldn't know her. My father was one

of the elders who put us out on the march
with our cooking pots and killing sticks

before he got ready to shake hands with death
in the war, the war that was always coming.

I was too little to carry a dang—
a pole with a hand grip, carved out of tree roots—

Khartoumers made fun of us, calling us stupid
stick-people, Tagbondo. *All that was long ago.*

. . .

I was six years old. I had only a shirt.
Lots of us dropped out along the way

recruited to join guerrilla bands,
given machetes, beer, even guns.

The oldest, sixteen. In the refugee camp
in Kakuma I learned English, team sports

shower and soap, fork and spoon.
I studied geography, read Lord Jim

and coached younger boys in basketball
a game made for Dinkas. Even skinny and homesick

we're the tallest tribe in the world, it is written.
The war never ended, the camp overflowed.

Some people from the UN came to see
the city of lost boys lodged in this settlement.

One of them sent me a pair of Nikes.
Nikes, my first shoes. The day those shoes came

I was King, let me tell you. King of the camp.

———

Framed against buildings, in gray suit-and-tie
tall handsome William, who's birthdayless

. . .

but guesses he's twenty-two or -three
a shipping clerk now in the Western world

says, *Truly my whole life I never knew*
where I would put my head down at night

what I would eat, what day I would eat it
what day my head would drop off my shoulders.

Now I am at my highest place yet.
I sleep without fear. I eat without hoarding

but I worry about all the other boys
of the Dinka clan I left behind

in the Kakuma camp with their useless dangs
and their cooking pots and no relatives

no kin to turn to as long as they live.

Identifying the Disappeared

The exiles have returned from safe cold places
with their resistance to forgetting, returned
with brush and spoon, sieve and dustpan
to bring back the bones of a child, which are become
the bones of a nesting bird; the lip of a clavicle
transformed into angel wings which want to be
its mother; skulls for uncle, father, brother
who soiled themselves and died in the Resistance.

It is another day to walk about
testing the earth for springy places to insert
their tools, another day to see what the dead
saw in that instant after the machete
severed the critical artery,
after the eye went milky and the soul
flew away in horror and the flesh retreated
in narrow strips, like ribbons, from the bone.

The exiles have come back. They are breaking
the sleep of earth, they are packing the dry shards
of the disappeared in cardboard cartons
Relief provides—wood is scarce here—

and still they store up the names of the murderers
who have put away their uniforms and persuasions
under the landmine of respectability,
the trigger, God willing, one day they will trip on.

Bringing Down the Birds

FOR CHRISTOPHER COKINOS

Does it make you wince to hear
how the last of the world's great auks
were scalded to death on the Newfoundland coast
in vats of boiling water so that
birdshot would not mutilate the feathers
that stuffed the mattress your great-grandparents
lay upon, begetting your forebears?

Are you uncomfortable reading how
the flocks of passenger pigeons
that closed over the sky like an eyelid
the millions that roared like thunder
like trains, like tornados were wiped out, expunged
in a free-for-all a hundred years gone?
Can you bear the metaphor in how it was done?

Pet pigeons, their eyelids sewn, were tied
to stools a few feet off the ground until
hordes of their kind swooped overhead.
Released, their downward flutter lured
the multitude who were smothered in nets

while trappers leaped among them
snapping their necks with pincers.
The feathers from fifty pigeons
added up to a pound of bedding.

Does it help to name the one-or-two-of-a-kind
Martha or Rollie and exhibit them in a zoo
a kindly zoo with moats in place of wire
or clone from fished-up bits of DNA
a creature rather like the creature
it had been, left to the whim of nature?

Would bringing the ivory bill back from deep woods
to a greenhouse earth placate the gods?
The harlequin-patterned Labrador duck
the dowdy heath hen, the gregarious Carolina parakeet
that once bloomed like daffodils in flight,
if science could reconstruct them, how long
would it take us logging and drilling and storing up
treasures to do them all in again?

Soldiers

Old-timers itchy from waiting for
the three-toed sloth to wake and turn their way,
sweaty from hiking with binoculars
and camera to glimpse the reclusive quetzal,

stiff-legged on the trail of the wattled bell bird,
the anteater, the boa constrictor, begin
under the eyes of their Costa Rican guide
to exchange the massive data of their days.

The beaches they stormed at Normandy,
Anzio, Saipan refill with flak
and thudding shells. One of them ferried
ordnance over the Burmese Hump.

Another lay fathoms deep in a submarine
under arctic ice. One, culled from the infantry,
was shipped to Los Alamos to begin
the secret life that led (shame mixed with pride)

to the Bomb. Called at last to attention
they stargaze to see, under the guide's supervision,
a termite tunnel that rises above their heads
to a bulbous nest alive with pale-bodied clones.

. . .

When birds peck a hole in the passage, the rosy-cheeked
chief biologist explains, one
of the soldier termites, rudely bitter to taste,
offers his head for the good of the tribe within

as these old soldiers did, though how many classmates
equally clever with rifle and swift with grenade pin
nevertheless were left among the dead.
Weary heroes, they dream themselves back

in the perilous nest of the last good war
and wake at dawn to the birds' territorial shrieks
they are pleased to interpret as music.

Capital Punishment

On the way to his death Benny Demps
complained about what had happened
backstage: when they couldn't raise a vein
in either arm they went to his groin
which also refused to yield and then
cut his leg open. It was bloody
said the 10 o'clock news on TV
but they finally made connection.

We are shown only the flat
uninhabited metal stretcher
but as the black curtain oozed upward
Benny went on calling for justice
from his tidy blue-sheeted gurney
demanding an investigation
into the pain they had caused him
the botch they had made of his exit.

Now we are given pictures
of victims in Sierra Leone.
The thing about the machete
is how quickly bone and gristle
will dull it, how often
you have to sit down and hone it

to hack off those hundreds of limbs
above or below the elbow.

One village elder was spared his thumbs.
On camera he holds out his arms
to show us what you can do
with two thumbs. Some
of the armless dripping blood
ran into the bush after their attackers
crying, *come back, I implore you!*
Come back and kill us, please kill us.

The newscast goes blank. Silver
streaks jitter across the screen
which finally fills with merciful snow.
Why are we shown mutilations
and denied execution? I long
to go back and hear out Benny Demps
taxing this vengeful world of slash
and burn and inject, I want

to be there for the last act
in his ruthless life, the scene
we were not permitted to witness,
his naïve six-minute diatribe
against the state, the vitriol
of his soliloquy running down
like a windup toy:
the gentleness of his exit.

Want

The world is awash in unwanted dogs:
look-alike yellow curly-tailed mongrels that come
collared and wormed, neutered and named, through customs
come immunized, racketing and rabies-tagged

to Midwestern farms from Save the Children, the Peace Corps
come from Oxfam into the carpeted bedrooms of embassies
into the Brooklyn lofts of CARE workers on leave
the London, Paris, Geneva homes of Doctors Without Borders

and still the streets of Asmara, Kigali, Bombay
refill with ur-dogs: those bred-back scavenging flea-ridden
sprung-ribbed bitches whose empty teats make known
the latest bitten-off litter of curs that go back to the Pleistocene.

And what of the big-headed stick-figured children naked
in the doorways of Goma, Luanda, Juba, Les Hants
or crouched in the dust of haphazard donkey-width tracks
that connect the named and the nameless hamlets of Want?

There will always be those who speed past unbeguiled.
There will always be somewhere a quorum of holy fools
who wade into the roiling sea despite the tsunami
to dip teaspoon after teaspoon from the ocean.

VI

The Long Marriage

The sweet jazz
of their college days
spools over them
where they lie
on the dark lake
of night growing
old unevenly:
the sexual thrill
of Peewee Russell's
clarinet; Jack
Teagarden's trombone
half syrup, half
sobbing slide;
Erroll Garner's
rusty hum-along
over the ivories;
and Glenn Miller's
plane going down
again before sleep
repossesses them . . .

Torschlusspanik.
Of course
the Germans have

a word for it,
the shutting of
the door,
the bowels' terror
that one will go
before
the other as
the clattering horse
hooves near.

Keeping in Touch

Either a series of minor earthquakes or
the weekly announcement of another
paroled rapist offsets the clement weather,

mimosas loosing showers of yellow pollen,
the worst of a series of offending allergens
in this graduate student cinderblock warren

where pipes burst and playgrounds overflow
and every aspiring Asian family makes do.
Three black-eyed toddlers under my window

trill back and forth in their mother tongue
scolding dolls they pick up and rock and abandon,
shake them, forgive them, rerock and put down

mornings when you call me long distance to report
it is 5 below in English and Fahrenheit
in New Hampshire, and I remember my high school part

in Thornton Wilder's one-act, "The Happy Journey
from Trenton to Camden"—thirty miles by early
auto—staged with wooden chairs to signify

. . .

the family coupe that sported running boards
as now 3,000 miles apart we prop our words
in place of touch, dial, redial, and hoard

absence with its pucker of California citrus
that comes between and yet keeps us.

Hark, Hark

The phones, the long-distance phones are ringing.
The satellite phone from the field camp in Kosovo.
The lawyer's phone in a complex in Palo Alto.
The car phone conveying a child to baseball practice.
In this way the siblings converse and condole

much as the now-vanished Carolina parakeets
with their sunflower-yellow heads
and kindergarten-green backs
swooped down to their captured kin
and fluttered all night in noisy flocks
against the cage, their opposing breasts
marked with the wire grids that kept them apart
until the last ornamental bird was extinguished

as we will be, but not without having first
listened in to the ongoing shrill, with all of its
anxieties and triumphs taking place among
the offspring we raised, pre-analog transmission
and the ones they are raising in a cacophony of connection.

The Joy of Cooking, 1931

In my smudge-thumbed
first edition

Irma Rombauer
says *It is*

a thrill to possess
shelves well stocked

with home-canned food.
Agreed.

And so we've picked
twenty pounds

of high fox grapes
twined around

a treed escarp
and lugged the pail

home, uphill.
In fact, she avers

. . .

you will find
their inspection

—often sur-
reptitious—

(The fat blue-bot-
tomed pot begins

to spit and pop.
It smells delicious.)

and the pleasure
of serving the fruit

of your labor
(I mash the burst

globes, let simmer.
The season cambers

toward winter.
Strain juice, measure,

reboil with sugar.
Upend jars

on covered table.)
comparable

. . .

only to a clear
conscience. Dear

Mrs. Rombauer,
time takes us singly

and ungently
down the jellied

slope to here.
When we're gone,

let sunlight shine
through jars and jars.

Wood

Every November we buy from the logger
a cord of trash wood, the green tops of weedy poplar
for the horses to gnaw on all winter, studiously stripping
the bark in long, juicy curls, thereby sparing
our fence boards from the deep curves
seen elsewhere on poor-mouth farms.
And then it is spring.
                  Dr. Green arrives
rich with dandelions, bromegrass, and clover.
The six-foot spindles of now-naked popples clutter
the paddock, the lawn, the roadside. You insist
they must be gathered and stacked to be sawn.
Someone can burn them, they make a quick fire.
As quick as newspaper, I say. I want to hurl them
into the gully. Let nature do the recycling.

Of course you win. After living so long a time
side by side, I know how to choose; what quarrels
not to pick.
            And so in the chartreuse days
of April we work together stacking by size
neat piles of trash wood to gladden the eye:
wood enough for the hereafter.

Domesticity

Oh, what a weak sticker, you groan, as the batter pops
out to the infield. We're propped
up in two beds—mine's electric, with crib
sides, rented to ease eleven broken ribs—
watching the Red Sox, who are in the cellar
and dozing between Demerol and errors.

You yawn, the resident optimist
no family should lack, always stitching
a selvedge along the silver lining
—the luck of my unbroken pelvis—
so that when in a bizarre twist
they tie it up in the bottom of the ninth
you crow, they're still alive and kicking!
We rouse as for the crisis of an old friend
and watch through extra innings to the end.

John Green Takes His Warner, New Hampshire, Neighbor to a Red Sox Game

Everett down the hill's
52 and trim. No beer gut.
Raises beef, corn, hay, cuts
cordwood between harvests.
Goes to bed at 8 and falls
into sleep like a parachutist.

He's never been to a ballgame.
He's never been to Boston though
he went over to Portland Maine
one time ten, fifteen years ago.

In Sullivan Square, they
luck out, find a space
for John's car, take
the T to Fenway Park.
The famous T!
A kind of underground trolley.
Runs in the dark.
No motorman that Ev can see.
Jammed with other sports fans.

John has to show him
how to put the token in.

How to press with his hips
to go through the turnstile.
How to stand back while
the doors whoosh shut.
How to grab a strap
as the car pitches forward.
How to push out
with the surging crowd.

Afterward Ev says the game's
a whole lot better on tv.
Too many fans.
Too many other folks for him.

Lying in Bed Away from Home

Cardinals outside this window ask *cheer what cheer*
as they did from childhood's oaks, their voices smeared

with Latin unguents from the Sisters of St. Joseph's
Mass next door till the fire station's braying riffs

and hoots uphill raised my father from his chair
to pursue the immense arsons of his desire

my unemployed uncles up front in the bile-green Packard
my teenage brothers asprawl in the back, and I anchored

at the window overlooking Carpenter Lane
as the hook-and-ladder flew past with all my male kin

giving chase as if to extract some mysterious essence
from the sorrows of those burned out or down for insurance.

What did I know, sent early to bed, girlchild
parched with my own small longings, how it was to thrill

to the luck of escape from the flames, to the whiff of sex
the siren gave off that sang them away from the redbirds' nest.

A Place by the Sea

... *bottomless perdition, there*
to dwell.

—JOHN MILTON

Now there is nothing, my father said, mock-groaning
as he wrote out the check for his taxes, between me
and a word I heard as Perdistant, a place possibly
next door to Atlantic City, that playground of sand and sins,
private nudist beaches, and even then, slot machines.

And did he arrive there, my father, after his third and final
heart attack, the EMTs pounding his chest
shouting Pete, Pete, come back, twirling the dials,
trying to jump-start his paltry machine with theirs?

And was it what I had pictured, the broadest and best
of vistas, when I the apprentice tried to decipher
the code of my parent, his hapless what-the-hell shrug
in the face of Perdistant, I his five-year-old daughter
climbing the tree of his torso to partake of his hug?

Flying

When Mother was little, all
that she knew about flying was what
her bearded grandfather told her:
every night your soul flies
out of your body and into
God's lap. He keeps it under
his handkerchief until morning.

Hearing this as a child haunted me.
I couldn't help sleeping.
I woke up each morning groping
as for a lost object lodged perhaps
between my legs, never knowing
what had been taken from me or what
had been returned to its harbor.

When as a new grandmother
my mother first flew cross-country
—the name of the airline escapes me
but the year was 1947—
she consigned her soul to the Coco-
Chanel-costumed stewardess
then ordered a straight-up martini.

. . .

As they landed, the nose wheel wobbled
and dropped away. Some people screamed.
My mother was not one of them
but her shoes—she had slipped them off—
somersaulted forward. Deplaning
she took out her handkerchief
and reclaimed her soul from the ashen stewardess.

That night in a room not her own
under eaves heavy with rain
and the rue of a disbelieving daughter
my mother described her grandfather to me
a passionate man who carried his soul
wedged deep in his pants' watch-pocket:
a pious man whose red beard had never seen scissors

who planted his carrots and beets
in the dark of the moon for good reason
and who, before I was born,
rose up like Elijah.
Flew straightaway up into heaven.

Giving Birth

FOR YANN, AT NINETEEN

Every month I went to the obstetrician. The sign
over his examining table said: Familiarity
Breeds. Every month I lay down on the hard slab
to be poked and peered at, or—this was before ultrasound—
palpated per rectum. Every month I answered
the same perfunctory questions:
any trouble with our waterworks? Are we sleeping?
Every month I was ushered out by Dr. Congeniality
as if this were indeed a joint enterprise
and not the singular journey I took three times.

No father was permitted to attend.
No mother to be conscious during the crossing.
Painkillers and truth serums were the drugs of choice.
I thrashed and swore furiously, I was told, ex post facto.
My vocabulary astonished the interns.
Thus Demeroled and scopolamined, my body
slammed through the waves without me
only taking me back in when a face
leaned over mine each time in the recovery room
and said, Congratulations. You have a girl.
You have a girl. You have a boy.

. · .

Even after landfall I was held in bed.
During the week-long stay in Maternity no infant
could cross the threshold of the four-mothers-to-a-room
except at feeding time. The medley
of sobbing babies being trundled up and down
the corridor at 6-10-2-6-10
swelled and subsided, tragic doppler music

so that when your mother nineteen years ago
asked me to be her birth partner, I swelled
with prestige. I went to birthing classes
for the breathing, the panting, the back rubs.
I packed special teas and lotions.
Ever efficient, she went into labor before my plane
had touched down on the far side of the Atlantic.

Darkness drifted on us from the mountains.
We drove to the hospital pausing between contractions.
The midwives—one spoke German,
the other, French—installed us in a bedroom
wallpapered with nosegays of roses.
No metal crib sides. No stirrups. Everyone
was eerily cheerful. The boyish doctor
strode in still clutching his motorcycle helmet
seemingly uneasy in this gathering of women,
content to be a bit player unless needed.

Painfully and with enormous effort your mother opened.
Mottled purple and black-haired, an unexpected

animal emerged from the tunnel. I gasped.
The midwives handed me this hard foreign muscle
that flexed and contracted from the shock of entry.
I held it in a shallow basin of warm water
and sloshed it with antiseptic soap to remove
the coating it had come with and then carried it
to the bed where it magicked into the baby
your mother had brought forth and now put to her breast.

You slept in the curl of your mother's body
as we four women drank champagne
and ate zweibach and congratulated each other.
At first light, driving your mother's little Renault
I followed the German-speaking midwife
back through the unfamiliar streets
back to the converted farmhouse overlooking
the border crossing where we honked farewells
and the sun came up unsurprised.

A Game of Nettles

Torture, we called it, stripped to the waist
three girl cousins nine and ten
who'd learned a light caress would break
the leaf tip sac and sting the skin

like summer's dreaded typhoid shots.
Whoever let go first was Out
and each of us contrived to lose
in the back fields of innocence

entire mornings in July.
We stroked the dark green hairy leaves
across our chests to feel the fuse
ignite our pale mysterious disks.

Tinctured with uneasiness
our nipples startled and leapt up.
Called in to lunch, washed, combed and dressed
we sat at table, little beasts

secretly burning inside our shirts
not knowing we had stumbled on
forbidden pleasures, adult sport,
not knowing we were masochists.

The Collection

In Gestapo-ridden Paris, Bertrand,
a boy I met once he was safe in Queens,
cruised the Metro nightly with a razor
blade concealed between his fingers
for harvesting sundry decorations
from the chests of sodden German soldiers.

Only child, too young to be a courier
in the Resistance, he spent the year he should
have been bar mitzvahed slept against,
felt up, and vomited on. He loved geometry
even then, at home in three dimensions,
grew up to be an astrophysicist.

No drama in the rest of Bertrand's life
spent measuring black holes, red giants,
could match the terror in the slither
of his fingers, the thrill of slicing
trophies from their moorings, then pocketing
the stash to add to his collection.

He brought it to the States in bonbon boxes,
one for ribbons and tinny iron crosses,
the other for thickly tarnished buttons,

and kept them in a knapsack under his bed.
High school seniors, we clung to each other
while his parents divorced, that year in Queens

but when I spent the night in Bertrand's bed
he unpacked and fondled his treasures
as if I were no longer there.

The Angel

You didn't have to be a Catholic mother
to march with the Catholic Mothers Against The War
and lie in front of the Navy Yard buses waiting

to ferry recruits to their berths in Boston Harbor.
You didn't have to be any kind of mother.
One was a priest, two others merely fathers.

You didn't have to have a war resister—
my 17-year-old son—to serve as adviser.
Arrested twice for civil disobedience,

he knew the holding pen they put us in,
30 middle-class and mostly Catholic women.
He stood up with his father and the bondsman.

The whole world was watching. Nothing I could
have done back then in self-righteousness
would have impeded my body's downward slippage.

I am too old now to go to jail for my conscience,
to wait to be processed, dismissed with a click
of the stapler. These days I take them by the hand,

. . .

each woman I walk to the door of the clinic
past the chants of *Murderer! Baby killer!* Who are
the harassers? My old compatriots' granddaughters?

What a long purgatory life is,
a tethered dog on the lawn next door forever
struggling against the circle he carves for himself,

wearing his claws to stubs in the hard pack,
awaiting the angel he summons with his bark,
the angel who comes at last to unfasten his collar.

VII

The Ancient Lady Poets

I, who alone survived, move through
my old age like a camera
in the hands of a hard-core realist
bending over knucklebones on the lawn
or the rot of a long-dead red squirrel
after the snow has melted.

The landscape of my body up close
is one of snags and glaciations.
You can see the path of a forest fire
that devoured one breast leaving
the other shyly hanging in space,
my still abundant hair whitening,
my almost bald pubis still useful.

We had planned to age elegantly.
The Japanese twins who lived to
one hundred and seven could not have
outdone us cruising Fifth Avenue in
our custom-made shoes, our handsome
obedient Dalmatians heeling beside us.

. . .

Hatless, earringed, no sign of scoliosis
we'd planned to stride forth block
after block, well-published, polished.

Bad girls of the New England Poetry Club
our wit and fame up ahead
leading a procession of disciples.

Three Dreams After a Suicide

—ANNE SEXTON, 1974

1.

We're gathered in the funeral home, your friends
who are not themselves especially friends,
with you laid out on view in the approved fashion
wearing the bright-red reading dress with cut-glass buttons
that wink at the ceiling, when you spring
like a jack-in-the-box from the coffin
crying Boo! I was only fooling!

2.

After the terrible whipping you are
oddly pleased with yourself,
an impenitent child, the winner.
It's Daddy Death who's quit.
Once more you've worn him out
from all his lifting and striking.
His belt lies shredded in his meaty fist.

3.

We are standing together in a sunless garden
in Rockport, Mass. I'm wearing the hat
the artist painted you in

and suddenly swarms of wasps
fly up under the downturned brim.

O death, where is thy sting?
Tar baby, it is stickered to me; you
were my wasp and I your jew.

Oblivion

The dozen ways they did it—
off a bridge, the back of a boat,
pills, head in the oven, or
wrapped in her mother's old mink coat
in the garage, a brick on the accelerator,
the Cougar's motor thrumming
while she crossed over.

What they left behind—
the outline of a stalled novel, diaries,
their best poems, the note that ends
now will you believe me,
offspring of various ages, spouses
who cared and weep and yet
admit relief now that it's over.

How they fester, the old details
held to the light like a stained-glass icon
—the shotgun in the mouth, the string
from toe to trigger; the tongue
a blue plum forced between his lips
when he hanged himself in her closet—
for us it is never over

       . . .

who raced to the scene, cut the noose,
pulled the bathtub plug on pink water,
broke windows, turned off the gas,
rode in the ambulance, only minutes later
to take the body blow of bad news.
We are trapped in the plot, every one.
Left behind, there is no oblivion.

Acknowledgments

Some of these poems have appeared, sometimes in slightly different form or under different titles, in the following publications:

Agni: "Capital Punishment," "William Remembers the Outbreak of Civil War"

Arts & Letters: "8 A.M. in Grays Point," "Opening the Doors of Perception in Grays Point," "The Woman Who Moans"

The Atlantic Monthly: "Oblivion"

The Boston Book Review: "Why There Will Always Be Thistle"

The Connecticut Review: "Flying," "Grady, Who Lost a Leg in Korea, Addresses Me in the Rehab Gym"

Country Journal: "Wood"

Epoch: "Soldiers," "The Ancient Lady Poets"

Five Points: "Grand Canyon," "The Greenhouse Effect," "Identifying the Disappeared"

The Georgia Review: "Bringing Down the Birds," "Hard Frost: On a Line by Hopkins," "Imagining Marianne Moore in the Butterfly Garden," "*The Joy of Cooking*, 1931," "Mother of Everyone," "My Life," "Want"

The Hudson Review: "Skinnydipping with William Wordsworth"

Kalliope: "A Game of Nettles"

The Maine Times: "Highway Hypothesis"

The Massachusetts Review: "The Exchange"

The Michigan Quarterly Review: "The Angel," "The Collection"

The New Yorker: "Ghazal: On the Table," which appeared as "On the Table," "Three Dreams After a Suicide"

Nightsun: "Domesticity"

Orbis (England): "A Place by the Sea"

Ploughshares: "Thinking of Gorki While Clearing a Trail," "Hark, Hark"
Poetry: "Lying in Bed Away from Home"
Poetry International: "Afoot in Grays Point," "Calling Out of
    Grays Point"
The Progressive: "The Politics of Bindweed," which appeared as
    "Poem for an Election Year: The Politics of Bindweed"
River City: "The Potato Sermon"
Washington Square: "Rilke Revisited"
Witness: "The Brown Mountain," "Pantoum, with Swan"

I am indebted to Bernard F. Scholz, Professor of Comparative Literature, Rijks Universiteit, Groningen, Netherlands, for providing the derivation of the word *torschlusspanik*: it "refers to the rush in and out just before the city gates were closed in the walled towns of the principalities which dotted Germany until Napoleon put an end to the 'Kleinstaaterei.'"

The late Anne Sexton wrote the phrase "Muriel, mother of everyone" in thanking Muriel Rukeyser for sending her a copy of *The Speed of Darkness*.

Aunt Sass
Christmas Stories

Aunt Sass
Christmas Stories

P. L. Travers

With a foreword by
Victoria Coren Mitchell

Illustrations by Gillian Tyler

hachette
BOOKS

NEW YORK   BOSTON

Copyright © by Trustees of the P. L. Travers Will Trust, 1941, 1943, 1944
Foreword copyright © Victoria Coren Mitchell, 2014
Illustrations copyright © Gillian Tyler, 2014

Each story in this collection was published in a limited edition of five hundred copies, privately printed for the friends of the author as a Christmas Greeting: *Aunt Sass*, first printed in the United States of America in 1941 by Reynal and Hitchcock, Inc. *Ah Wong*, first printed in the United States of America in 1943 by The High Grade Press *Johnny Delaney*, first printed in the United States of America in 1944 by The High Grade Press.

This edition published in Great Britain in 2014 by Virago Press.

Hachette Books
Hachette Book Group
1290 Avenue of the Americas
New York, NY 10104
www.HachetteBookGroup.com

Printed in the United States of America

RRD

First Hachette Books edition: October 2015

10 9 8 7 6 5 4 3 2 1

Hachette Books is a division of Hachette Book Group, Inc.
The Hachette Books name and logo are trademarks of
Hachette Book Group, Inc.

The publisher is not responsible for websites (or their content)
that are not owned by the publisher.

ISBN 978-0-316-38658-6
LCCN 2015945309

Contents

Foreword

These stories should be a delight for any reader, but particularly magical for fans of P. L. Travers' great masterpiece, the *Mary Poppins* stories. Many of the preoccupations of those wonderful novels appear in these pages: merry-go-rounds, gorgon nurses, small dogs, smart hats, suns and moons and comets and constellations.

The spirit is there too, and many of the ideas: predominantly, that children know darkness. P. L. Travers disliked the Disney version of *Mary*

Poppins because she found it too cartoonish and sunny. Her own books made room for the fear and sadness of children, their natural and tragic awareness of impermanence. As she says here, in the story of *Johnny Delaney*: 'Children have strong and deep emotions but no mechanism to deal with them.'

Because these tales were printed privately as Christmas gifts for the author's friends and family, and because of their tone, one assumes that they are autobiographical. There is some poetic licence but P. L. Travers, who had a keen sense of the spiritual and often dreamed of worlds beyond this one, might not approve of such literal distinctions.

For example, in *Ah Wong* Travers explores (as she does so often in the famous nanny novels) the deep unknowability of people. What may read as racial discrimination today bespeaks a fascination with difference, rather than a rejection of it. The story's end is deeply moving; is it true? Did the young Travers (then Helen Lyndon Goff) really, in later life, meet an old Chinese cook from her childhood on his deathbed? Was there ever such poetic closure? In her genuine Australian childhood, her father worked in a bank rather than a sugar plantation. Travers added the spoonful of sugar, and possibly a lot more, but it doesn't matter. The magical, tragical and real have always been mixed up in her work.

It is the story of *Aunt Sass* that will bring the most joy to Poppins fans, offering clues to the inspiration for that immortal character. Aunt Sass (surely a version, if not an exact portrait, of Travers' own great-aunt Ellie) is a grand, sharp, mysterious and contradictory woman, 'stern and tender, secret and proud, anonymous and loving'. Like Mary Poppins, she twinkles and snaps in spits and spots.

It seemed to me, when I was researching P. L. Travers for a documentary, that the great author was just such a woman herself. She loved her adopted son and grandchildren deeply, but refused to express this in a sentimental or traditionally maternal way. She brought her granddaughter to live with her for several years – and yet, at home in London, she once refused entry to her daughter-in-law and infant grandchild because it was lunch-time.

Travers was 'secret and proud', certainly. She relished her public success and occasionally gave interviews, but then hated to be asked about either her own life or the genesis of *Mary Poppins*. She felt that this got in the way of the story. She preferred to suggest that everything came from the stars. I almost felt guilty reading the following Christmas-gift chronicles, redolent with childhood truth in the feeling, if not every last detail, but it was the guilt one feels when gobbling a delicious cake. Nothing so tempting could possibly have been left on the plate.

Of Aunt Sass, Travers writes beautifully: 'The sleepless humanity behind that crusty exterior reached out to every heart that came in contact with her.'

It is clear that a sleepless humanity surged in the breast of P. L. Travers, expressing itself in a myriad of wondrous characters, and no heart that's come into contact with her writing could remain untouched by it. I feel I know her better for reading these three stories, though she didn't necessarily want to be known better. I suspect that she, like Aunt Sass and Mary Poppins, was challenging to love – but, to my mind, all the more lovable for it.

Victoria Coren Mitchell, 2014

Aunt Sass

To Eugene and Curtice

H er name was Christina Saraset. She was a very remarkable person. Her remarkableness lay in the extraordinary and, to me, enchanting discrepancy between her external behaviour and her inner self. Imagine a bulldog whose ferocious exterior covers a heart tender to the point of sentimentality and you have Christina Saraset.

She was my great-aunt and the oldest person I ever met. This is hardly surprising since she was born in 1846 and died last year at the age of ninety-four, grievously disappointed that she could not make the century. Her life, both in the living and the recounting of it was, in the eyes of her family, compact of adventure and romance. Only those six years were lacking to make the picture complete.

It was in 1844 that my great-grandfather, with his young wife, sailed from England to Australia to recover health after a long illness. On arrival he made a prompt recovery, seized a huge tract of virgin forest with the grandiose simplicity of a robber baron, and built himself a mansion in the wilderness. Whether he really intended to live there nobody now knows, but the biennial appearance of the inevitable new baby compelled him to settle down. Soon there was a large Victorian family growing up among the Bushmen in rugged, pioneering splendour. Christina headed the list.

It was at her instigation that all the children were sent backward and forward on the voyage between Australia and England to be educated. 'I refuse to be brought up like a Savage!' she is reported to have said. And her father, already sensing the bulldog in her, hastened to charter a vessel. Aunt Sass, as we all called her, would remember for her numerous great-nieces and nephews wonderful excursions when a ship took three months sailing to England; when there was no Suez Canal; and the desert between the Red Sea and the Mediterranean had to be crossed on muleback.

Her stories of those days, like all her reminiscences, were original and intensely personal. There was little in them of the beauties of nature or the joys of youth. They were pithy tracts of moral behaviour and solid fact. Right and wrong were Aunt Sass's favourite subjects. Her remembrance of the Sphinx was that 'the huge ugly thing terrified your Great-aunt Jane. They had no right to put it there – just where people are passing!' Of the Pyramids, all she had to say was that 'your Great-uncle Robert was disappointed that they were not larger'. And all the glories of Sydney Harbour were as nothing compared to the fact that 'your great-grandfather lost a silver crown-piece in it one day when he was out sailing'. I used to think of the harbour floor as paved with silver because of Great-grandfather's coin.

That was Aunt Sass. Everything in the world came back to herself – or her family. She used notable people simply as a background for her own life. Her family was hung about with great occasions as Indians with wampum. The universe and the outer unknown worlds swung about the central pivot of Aunt Sass and those nearest her. She numbered among her friends many of the great figures of her time but she saw them not as creatures of history or fate, merely as beings whose human significance lay in their intimate relation to herself. Thus Disraeli was less a statesman than the man who rode to hounds beside her 'in yellow trousers and black-button-boots'. And Queen Victoria, for all Aunt Sass's ardent royalism, was chiefly remarkable for the fact that she preferred salt on her oatmeal to sugar, 'just like your great-grandmother'.

Her historical facts were equally piquant and irrelevant. Having presided, as it were, almost at the inception of a great commonwealth, the things she remembered best were its small domestic oddities. That fish and milk carts were drawn by dogs because of the scarcity of horses; and that people going out to dinner parties, 'even to Government House', carried their own bread with them. She never explained the reason for the latter custom and it was not till later that the vision of Aunt Sass setting out for Government House, all lace and taffeta, with a loaf of bread under one arm, ceased to be funny. Brooding over her reminiscences I realised that in those days the clearings in the bush must still have been small and scanty. Much time and energy are necessary to make wattle and eucalyptus give way to wheat and rye. Bread, therefore, must have been infinitely precious.

But most exciting of her reminiscences was one that told how, wine being costly and difficult to obtain, many low persons – of whom Aunt Sass could have known only by hearsay – drank methylated spirits. And this to such excess that they had only to strike a match for their lips to flare up in blue flame. 'And many of them,' Aunt Sass would conclude disgustedly, 'many of them *women*!' We trembled deliciously at the picture, imagining row upon row of women burning like candles in their doorways.

Aunt Sass, it was rumoured, had once been in love – with a prominent member of the government of that day. He was her cousin and for this reason, it was said, she would not, or felt she could not, marry him. Nobody knew the rights of this story for she kept her own secrets closely. The rumour and the pictures it projected were springboards for innumerable family witticisms. Aunt Sass in love – think of it! Nevertheless, for me there was something about her, something that breathed through the tough outer body – an air, a scent, a whisper – the unmistakable essence of one whom love has struck on the heart. Occasionally, in an old barn, you become aware, though the scent has long since vanished, that once there were apples in the loft. Aunt Sass was like that.

But though she remained unmarried, her spinsterhood never succeeded in damming up her activities. She was a born ancestress and matriarch and used the children and grandchildren of her brothers and sisters for her own dynastic purposes. Each new child was taken to be looked over by Aunt Sass much as the children of old were carried to the Temple to be blessed. If the child pleased her, its future was assured.

In spite of the fact that she had two brothers, Aunt Sass assumed the position and privileges of head of the family when her father died and retained them until she herself followed him to the vault. She was like the central shaft of a merry-go-round. When her whistle blew the family revolved about her like so many wooden horses. Only the hardiest had courage to flout that fierce face and the deep voice like the sound of a bass viol. But these had their reward for they were the ones who came nearest to her heart. She respected courage above all things and from behind that belligerent exterior would watch it with a heart melting with pride and gentleness. But if anybody hinted at the existence of such sentiment she would go to the most devious lengths to deny it. She not only did good and blushed to find it fame, she did good and was ready to vilify anybody who discovered it.

It was her habit to disapprove of all suggestions and projects on principle. 'Idiotic nonsense!' she would shout. But as likely as not would send a cheque for the furthering of them. She calmly disinherited a great-niece of four because the child, kissing her goodnight, remarked, 'Oh, Aunt Sass, your moustache does prick!' But she balanced fate by showering the delinquent with such gifts that when Aunt Sass died the disinherited one was found to have received more than her rightful share.

'I never mention anything I want in front of your Aunt Sass,' Great-aunt Jane used to say, 'because she merely says "Don't be a fool, Jane!" and rushes out to buy it for me.'

Aunt Sass had only to hear of somebody in trouble to remark with almost gleeful callousness and that curious convulsion in her nose that was something between a snort and a sniff, 'Well, they've made their bed, let them lie on it!' Thereafter, having thus presented herself as a complete harpy, she would secretly set about making the bed as comfortable as possible.

She was already ancient when I was born; had embedded herself in the social life of two countries, England and Australia; had made the journey between them seventeen times; amassed unlimited friends and memories; broken her hip and mended it at the age of sixty-five and written her reminiscences. Later, when these came into my hands, I begged her to have them published. She reared and snorted like an angry horse. 'Published! Don't be a fool. They were written to please myself, not for strange persons in book-stalls. What! *You* put me in a book! I trust you will never so far forget yourself as to do anything so vulgarly disrespectful!' Sniff, sniff.

From the first she was for me a figure of romance. She had a tall, gaunt, graceless frame, a grim face with a long upper lip that curled at the corners when she smiled, and a voice like the Father Bear's voice in the story of Goldilocks. Her face was exactly like her character, definite, sharply outlined, with no suggestion of muzziness. Steering a path between good and evil had no dangers for Aunt Sass. Everything was black and white; grey had no place in her world. I saw her as somebody very near to God, the only person who appeared to be in His confidence. He and Aunt Sass were always right and woe betide anybody who thought differently!

As far as Aunt Sass was concerned, the best things had already happened. And of course they had happened to her. The most notable experiences, the handsomest people, the grandest festivities, the gloomiest funerals – all had congregated to Aunt Sass. It was her fixed conviction that there was nothing left for anybody else. The future, as she saw it, was a constantly diminishing return.

After recounting some incident in her career she would fold it up, as it were, and lock it away in her own private safe with the contemptuous conclusion – 'I can hardly imagine anything so interesting is likely to happen to *you*!' If one commented admiringly upon any of her possessions, or praised one of the photographs that stood in close military formation on piano, mantelpiece or table, she would retort – 'Well may you say so! Quite the most beautiful person (or object) *you* are ever likely to see!'

What was wrong with our eyes, we wondered?

What, indeed, was wrong with life that it had allowed Aunt Sass to use up all the best bits before we arrived? It was not until we grew older that we began to perceive that in spite of Aunt Sass's appalling rightness, there might still be something left.

But that very rightness, coupled with her fierceness, was a wonderful adventure for a child. The grim face was stony with conviction, the deep voice rumbled and you felt a delicious tremor of fear and anticipation fly through you. Any minute, any second, some terrible miracle might happen. *Would* the world fall in two if you brought her the wrong knitting needles? *Would* you go up in smoke if you tweaked Tinker's tail or Badger's ear? (She kept a succession of small dogs, two by two, and the pairs were always called Tinker and Badger, inheriting the names as though they were titles.) The terror and delight of that strange manner infected all children and they adored her as something more than human. She issued orders as

though she were a general at the War Office and spit-spot, off you went, trembling, to carry them out or perish. Sometimes she would communicate with you in doggerel verse made up on the spot, her voice rumbling and her eyes snapping ominously.

> I looked through the window and what did I
> see?
> A bad little boy who wouldn't eat his Tea.

I said 'I will spank him and send him to bed!'
                    (Pause for effect.)
But I gave him a *large* Chocolate Drop instead.

Or she would give her own sudden unexpected twist to nursery rhymes, far more exciting than the known and expected rythm.

Little Bo-Peep has lost her sheep
And can't tell where to find them,
Leave them alone and they'll come home
Saying '*What a thoroughly careless little girl!*'

or

Augustus was a chubby lad
Fat ruddy cheeks Augustus had
And everybody saw with joy
*The disgustingly overfed unhealthy-looking
        child!*

Every time a new baby came to our family I, being the eldest, was sent to Aunt Sass. Whether as a means of preserving the other children or as a treat for myself, I never found out. But treat it was. It was a long overnight journey. After the guard had put me to bed on the luggage-rack in his van I would lie listening to the train shrieking its lonely whistle through the lonely bushland, seeing it cutting its own way through the forests, feeling that its sole purpose was to carry me safely to Aunt Sass. It was as though she, all-powerful, had sent the train for me. It was an iron thread, a fiery necklace stretched between the bulky body of my mother and the skinny frame of Aunt Sass. And always at the end of the journey, there she would be – the tall belligerent figure faithfully waiting, an ivory and ebony stick in its hand, a hat with two pigeon's wings on its head. One wing would have been enough for anybody else. Aunt Sass had to have two.

The greeting was always the same. 'Hurrumph, here you are at last! The train was half a minute late. Very careless. Now, I trust you will be a well-behaved little girl and give Elizabeth no trouble.' Elizabeth was her personal maid, as old as Aunt Sass and even more gaunt and forbidding, and during my visits she performed the duties of nurse. Performed is the exact word, for it was a complete vaudeville act. Elizabeth brushed my hair till it fell out, scrubbed my face till it bled, tweaked and pinched me into my clothes and spoke of these maltreatments as her 'daily burden'. *Her* daily burden! I was very glad when Elizabeth died.

The only time the greeting varied was when the hat fell off as Aunt Sass bent to kiss me. She jammed it brutally back upon her head with the pigeon's feathers facing the wrong way and said to me furiously, 'Why didn't you remind me to wear my hatpins!'

Living with Aunt Sass was a precarious adventure. When you were old enough you took luncheon with her every day. Her appetite was so large that it was always touch and go whether there would be any of the best things left for you. Often I have been thankful to get the bare bones from the stew. I once saw her eat a dozen peaches at a sitting. She then took up the last remaining peach, remarked loudly to herself, 'Well, it's hardly worth while leaving *one*!' and finished that, too. 'You,' she said to me, 'may take an apple. Apples are good for the teeth.'

A houseful of servants revolved about Aunt Sass, forming a sort of inner circle within the larger one of the family. In spite of these she always insisted on washing the best china herself after tea. 'In order to preserve it!' she explained, though she never failed to chip off a handle or crack a saucer. She also made her own marmalade for no better reason than that her mother had done so before her. Shrouded in an enormous apron, she would stand over the pan stirring the yellow mess, spilling it over the stove and blaming the cook for the stove being there to be spilt on. It was a nauseous con-coction, tasting of burnt peel and, oddly enough, carrots. But as an honour Aunt Sass classed it with the V.C. or the Ribbon of the Garter and nobody, except herself (she never touched marmalade!), was game to refuse it at breakfast. Her friends, also, were presumed to have received something in the nature of a knighthood when a pot was presented to them. Time and again I have sat with Aunt Sass when she opened her letters and heard her remark 'Mrs Belmore thanks me for my *delicious* marmalade,' or 'Such *satisfying* conserve, says Colonel Whyte-Thompson.' I used to wonder what Mrs Belmore and the Colonel did with it, and where they would go when they died.

Aunt Sass could never forgive a tale-telling child. Yet she herself was one of the greatest gossips that ever breathed. Nobody's affairs were safe from her. She could keep an *essential* secret royally but could never resist speeding a rumour on its way. It was a point of honour with her to do so, rather as one redirects carrier pigeons that land on one's lawn. I once heard her telephone twenty-five people in one evening to acquaint them with the news of a distant relative's runaway marriage.

'Marry in haste and repent at leisure – that's what *I* say!' she remarked gleefully at the end of each conversation, having left the reputation of the couple in shreds. The next day, however, I was ordered to pack up a dozen pots of marmalade to be despatched to them special delivery and was nearly disinherited for discovering under the smallest pot a large cheque made out to the lovers.

When it came to argument, particularly argument between the sexes, Aunt Sass had a profound conviction that all women – with the single exception of herself – were wrong and all men splendidly right. If anybody had charged her with the incontrovertible fact that her greatest and most subtle kindnesses were to women, she would have snorted and made the excuse that women, being lesser creatures, needed it more. I remember coming back from one of my grim walks with Elizabeth and remarking inadvertently that *three* verses of 'God Save the King' were played as we passed the church.

'Stuff!' said Aunt Sass. 'Don't stand there like an idiot talking such stupid nonsense. They *never* play three verses of "God Save the King".'

'But they did today, Miss Sass!' Elizabeth supplemented inexorably.

'Hold your tongue, Elizabeth! You and the child are a pair of silly females. There's the doorbell. It's probably Major Caraway.'

And Major Caraway it was, cautiously tottering in on his withered old legs.

'Miss Saraset, Miss Saraset,' he quavered eagerly, 'I've just dropped in on my way from church and—'

'Major! Did they or did they *not* play three verses of "God Save the King"?' Aunt Sass looked at Elizabeth and me triumphantly, ready to confound us.

'Oh, indeed they *did*, Miss Saraset. And so beautifully, so moving, so—'

'I quite agree, Major! *Very* beautiful. Especially the second verse!' Aunt Sass's *volte-face* was almost girlishly gay, though privately she flashed me a warning glare that defied me to say 'I told you so!'

'But tell me, Major,' she went on archly, *'why* did they play three verses?'

'Why? But haven't you heard, Miss Saraset? Why – peace has been declared!'

Peace! The two pairs of old eyes gazed at each other and the old mouths stiffened to hide their trembling. Peace! Now with childhood behind me I can imagine their thoughts. The silent communications of Miss Saraset and Major Caraway. 'For the little time that is left,' said their eyes, 'we can sit in the sun without fear. No more sons and nephews will be taken from us, no more beautiful, bright young men. We will sit quietly, healing ourselves of the ones we have lost, watching the grandchildren growing and life settling again into a pattern we can understand.' I am part of that pattern now and can look back over its jagged bitter shapes to the hope they had for it. But at that time their emotion was quite incomprehensible. To the children the war was a place rather than an activity, the place towards which handsome young men with feathers in their hats marched through the streets and went aboard waiting ships. What could be the matter with Aunt Sass and the Major? Look – tears in their eyes!

'Elizabeth!' growled Aunt Sass. 'A bottle of wine and four glasses!'

When the wine came she filled three goblets, one for the Major, one for Elizabeth and one for herself. Then she poured a red trickle into the fourth. 'Drink, child,' she said gruffly, her eyes gentle with tears, 'drink, for the peace is for you!' And then, lest that glance should have been perceived or, worse still, comprehended, she added fiercely, 'And kindly do not spill it on that frock!'

A casual observer, meeting Aunt Sass for the first time, might have been excused for assuming that such a grim bulldog of an old lady could have hardly a friend to her name. But the fact was that she was surrounded by literally hundreds of people to whom she was, though she seemed quite unaware of it, an object of adoration. When she came downstairs for the first time after breaking her hip she had to slash her way with a stick through a thick jungle of flowers. Her old post-man was reported to have put in a yearly application for a larger pension because of the extra labour of carrying Aunt Sass's correspond-ence. Once, at a race meeting, I saw part of the crowd suddenly leave the rails in the middle of a race and rush towards the green. Thinking it was either royalty or an accident, I rushed too. But it was only a very old lady stalking across the grass on the arm of a Jockey Club steward, growling out greetings as she came. Miss Christina Saraset had decided, after twenty years of seclusion, to go to the Races!

None of these people, perhaps, could have explained why they loved her. She had no imagin-ation in the accepted sense, no graceful phrases. The best she could say of a beautiful person or a lovely object was 'Pretty!' Yet the sleepless human-ity hidden behind that crusty exterior reached out to every heart that came in contact with her. The gruff words were immediately discounted by the smile that lit the grim face with a radiance more moving than beauty.

Her reaction to suffering and sorrow was direct and complete. Inarticulate in words, she was richly articulate when it came to deeds. When my father died suddenly, leaving a nursery full of young children, she travelled seven hundred miles through scorching sub-tropical country to my mother, that beloved niece whom she herself had brought up from babyhood.

'Meg!' she said. It was all she knew how to say but I saw her face as the two women tenderly embraced. The little chestnut head went down on the gaunt square shoulder. Above it bent the sparse grey head and the face ravaged with sorrow and compassion. In the cool shadowy hall, smelling of sunlight and flowers, that look of hers told me what perhaps I already knew – that in the face of death there is nothing to be said.

Perhaps, indeed, there is nothing to be said about anything.

'You and the children will come to me!' She shook herself and gave the order like a sergeant on parade. And my mother merely nodded obediently and began to pack. A week later we were all in Aunt Sass's front hall being warned against knocking over the marble bust of Sir Walter Scott ('given by him to your great-grandfather'), to refrain from picking at the wallpaper ('one of the best *you're* ever likely to see!') and on no account to startle or annoy the reigning Tinker and Badger. The next thing we knew we were all sitting around the luncheon table hearing Aunt Sass descant unfavourably on our table manners, upbringing, personal appearance and ghastly futures. One after another the children melted into tears and were ordered from the table. Eventually, my mother could bear it no longer and left the room, weeping. I alone remained. She glared at me and through a maddening haze of tears I glared back.

'And now, I suppose, *you'll* break down and go, too!' she said jeeringly, taking the last handful of cherries.

'I will not, you old Beast!' I shouted to her. 'I'm not crying, it's only my eyes!'

At that I saw the light kindle in the fierce old face, a leaping joy at finding an adversary that would stand up to her and not give one inch of ground.

'Here,' she said, 'take the cherries to the little ones and tell your mother Aunt Sass is a bitter old woman and that she didn't mean a word of it.'

'I will take the cherries,' I said, 'but I will *never* forgive you, *ever*!'

The light flickered again. After that it never went out between us. For the rest of her life we fought with all the bitterness of true affection.

'I'll not go out with you in that hat!'

'Very well, Aunt Sass. I'll go by myself!' A pause.

'Why do you have to turn yourself into a

monstrosity? I'm ashamed to be seen with you. Get into the car!'

And later: 'Writing? Faugh! Why can't you leave that to journalists!' And then, grudgingly, 'You probably get it from my great-uncle Edward. He wrote a book of religious sonnets, privately printed at his own expense.'

I spurned Great-great-great-uncle Edward. If it had to come from somewhere, though I could not see why, I was in favour of my father.

'Don't be an idiot!' she spluttered. 'Ireland! Nothing but rain and rebels and a gabble of Gaelic. You couldn't have got it from *there*!' Then, with unwilling interest, 'Will you do it by hand or shall I give you a typing machine?'

Later still: 'What's all this I hear about you going to England? Ridiculous nonsense! You were always a fool. Well, how much is the fare – I'll send you a cheque for it!'

It was in England that I saw her for the last time. She took her last sea-voyage for the wedding of a great-niece. She was then ninety and I was shocked to find that the tall dominating woman had shrunk to the level of my shoulder. She looked like a little old witch. Where was the giantess, the frightening fairy-tale figure who in my childhood had seemed immense enough to knock against the stars and hold counsel with God? Gone for ever, down the hill towards death. Her native quality, however, was unshrinkable, and the family had to use force to prevent her cutting the cake herself with the bridegroom's sword.

It was on this occasion that I took her the first results of her gift of a 'typing machine'. She took the book in her hand and regarded it long and silently, smoothing it over and over with her stiff straight fingers. Then she opened it and looked at the dedication – in memory of my mother – and turned away sharply so that I should not see her face. 'She would have been pleased. My Meg would have been pleased,' she said gruffly. Then, facing me with all her old fierceness, 'The cover's pretty enough. I trust the inside is as good!'

(Oh, Aunt Sass, do you think you can fool me still? Sitting there glaring, defying me to the end? I know you, Christina Saraset – you naked and vulnerable inside the horny armour! You small and desolate in the straight-backed chair, shaken by the movement of life. You are not crying, are you, Christina – it is only your eyes!)

She took the book and put it aside to read in private, away from my searching gaze. I never saw her again. She set out next day for Australia. Something must have happened to her on that voyage; for it was when she arrived at her homeland that the change came. For the first time in her life she fell ill. It was not a real illness, merely old age. But it stretched her on her bed and drew a curtain of unconsciousness over her. We waited for news of the end.

Then, as suddenly and irrelevantly, she rallied. Death itself was no match for Aunt Sass. She woke up, saw the sunlight and began life again.

'She'll top the century after all!' said a hopeful great-nephew.

But the Aunt Sass who woke up was a new one on us all. The old gruffness, the fierce egotism were gone. She was concerned and anxious now to reveal the heart that had hidden so long behind it. It was as if, knowing her time to be short, she must hasten to let the light appear through the thinning crust of flesh. We had always been aware of the light but now it was she, the secret one, who was anxious to reveal it. That stretch of dark unconsciousness had taught her how not to be self-conscious. Her defences were down at last.

Letter after letter came to England, passionate in pride and tenderness, more like the notes of a lover than the usual communications of a great-aunt. They were the eager, stumbling phrases of one who having long been dumb, at length finds his voice. We shared them among us, marvelling. What would Aunt Sass do next?

The last was written to that sister 'your Great-aunt Jane' whom of all people in the world she had most tenderly loved. It said in closing—

The moon is coming up behind the wattle trees. Spreading and beautiful. It is almost as bright as the sun. Soon it will fill the whole harbour with its light. I love you all. I have had a long and happy life. God bless you. Goodnight.

The writing trailed away at the end in a waving line like the path of a comet. She died as her hand left the paper. And with her died something that the world will not gladly lose, something strong and faithful and tender. A human being that had cast off its rough outer skin to stand forth at last in beauty. A mind that was proud and incorruptible and a heart compact of love.

When I heard of it, I thought to myself, 'Some day, in spite of her, I shall commit the "disrespectful vulgarity" of putting Aunt Sass in a book.'

And then it occurred to me that this had already been done, though unconsciously and without intent. We write more than we know we are writing. We do not guess at the roots that made our fruit. I suddenly realised that there *is* a book through which Aunt Sass, stern and tender, secret and proud, anonymous and loving, stalks with her silent feet.

You will find her occasionally in the pages of *Mary Poppins*.

Ah Wong

To these children for Christmas

Greg and Susanna Coward,
Pamela and William Russell,
Richard and Ann Orage,
Miranda, Jane and Julian Mackintosh,
Eric and Anthony Reynal,
Joan and John Hitchcock,
Judith and Simon Stanton,
Angela Reeves
and
John Camillus Travers

I was ten when I first met him. The place was a sugar plantation in the tropics of Australia, and the day juts out like a promontory from the level lands of memory. It is linked with another important occasion, the day when Sam Foo dropped the pan of boiling fat on his foot. That, too, was something to remember. For it meant the end of tapioca pudding.

But I must begin at the beginning. At that time it was customary to have Chinese cooks on the plantations, and for a year we had suffered from the ministrations of Sam Foo. We never knew whether he thought white children really throve on an almost daily diet of tapioca or whether he was just plain lazy. Whichever it was, justice was at last meted out to him. An invisible avenging angel tipped the pan sideways one day and the next thing we knew Sam Foo, recumbent on a stretcher, was being carried through the cane-fields to an ambulance. Amid general acclamation he departed, shrieking with anguish.

But the loss of a cook in those outlying parts is fun only for the children. The cane was ready for cutting and not a man could be spared from the fields. The lubras (aboriginal women) shied away from the cook-stove as though its flames were the tongues of the devil. That left only our mother and Kate Clancy, the Irish nurse – both of them as temperamental, as far as cooking went, as any Hollywood star. After a succession of meals cooked by them it was possible to think of Sam Foo with kindness – even nostalgia.

Then one day, apparently out of nowhere, Ah Wong walked in. He was thin, where Sam had been fat; he was old and wrinkled where Sam had been young and moon-faced. Sam had waddled; Ah Wong had a light tripping step that was almost a run. But the distinctions did not end there. The most wonderful difference was that from under Ah Wong's hat there swung, long and black and shiny, a pigtail. Sam Foo had been short-haired, a modern Chinese. But here was a Chinese out of a fairy story.

'Melly Clismus!' he remarked in greeting, though Christmas was long past. 'Me Ah Wong. Me sit-down this place, bake-im, cook-im.'

The family stared at him as if he were a mirage. He tripped past it into the kitchen, put on one of Sam's aprons, and began to scramble eggs.

We watched him greedily. 'Do you believe in tapioca?' some child asked anxiously.

Ah Wong blinked his eyelids in delicate disdain. 'Tapiokee? What for? Him bin plenty bellyache. No tapiokee!'

Thus it was that Ah Wong walked into our lives and hearts. Within a week he had become the centre of the household, the small, high-powered dynamo that set us all in motion. For Ah Wong did not merely cook for the family. It soon became apparent that he owned the family. He darted like lightning about the house, dusting, making beds, sweeping and polishing. Ornaments and furniture were reshuffled and arranged according to Ah Wong's taste, and his tidiness in our sprawling, untidy house was very like a miracle.

'Missus bin leave flower-hat on floor, flower-hat bin plenty no good no more!' he would remark sternly, popping the hat into its box. And our mother would make earnest efforts to be tidy and please him.

If a baby cried, Ah Wong was always first at the crib. 'Now, now!' he would say. 'What you want, you bad-fellow small infant!' Then would follow a string of threats delivered in such soothing accents that the child immediately went to sleep again.

Even the garden, a sickly graveyard under Sam Foo, lifted its head for Ah Wong. Flowers bloomed, green rows of vegetables appeared, watermelons swelled like balloons. It was our belief that Ah Wong blew them up at night.

The only one of the household he never quite convinced was Kate Clancy. She spoke of him as 'that heathen idol' and treated him with contemptuous condescension. But she did not scruple to pile work that was rightfully hers upon his shoulders. It was Ah Wong who starched the frills and laces worn by our unfortunate generation, until our clothes stood out from our bodies like boards. It was Ah Wong who watched for the first hints of malaria in the rainy season. One shiver and quinine from the black bottle would be spooned into our mouths. If we refused the bitter draught his eyes would flash threateningly.

'You wanta make-im dead? All-along underground? Give Ah Wong big-mob bellyache here?' he would cry, slapping his hand dramatically over his heart till we gave in and swallowed.

Where, we wondered, had Ah Wong learned his

persuasive secrets. We never knew. Nor did he ever give us an inkling as to why he had come to us. Perhaps Sam Foo, convalescing in Cooktown, had told him the job was vacant. What did it matter? We needed him and he came. That, for the children, was enough. It was obvious that he had had some experience of the aboriginal part of Australia for he spoke English with the same intonation and singsong phrases that the black-fellows use. But beyond guessing at that we knew nothing.

His consistent answer, whenever anybody enquired into his past, was – 'Me come from China. Velly good place.' That was the final word. He never elaborated. Once we asked him what he thought of the Japanese. Even in those days the projected 'Japanese invasion' was common conversational currency in Australia.

I shall never forget Ah Wong's face when we asked him that. His eyes shrank and darkened until they were small black holes in his face. He fixed them upon us with passion, as though the question had outraged his inmost heart. He said nothing. But he pursed up his mouth into a terrible O and – suddenly – he spat. Full and round and venomous, his contempt dropped sizzling upon the hot planks of the veranda.

Deeply impressed, we gazed at it. To us it seemed the *only* comment upon Japan. So, swizzling the saliva round our mouths, we spat, too. Immediately the staring idol sprang to life.

'You big-mob bad-fellow childens! Spittee like that! Wheresa manners? My word, I tell-im Boss. Boss'll make-im plenty hiding. Smack-smack, the bottom!' And he looked down with shocked disdain at our little dribbles of spit drying beside his own.

He was proud of us, however, particularly the girls. He distinguished between myself and my sister by calling us Big-fellow Little Missy and Small-fellow Little Missy and continually assured our mother that we would fetch good prices when the time came to sell us in the market.

'I make-im fat,' he promised her. 'Bimeby, all-along fourteen, they fetcha ninety pounds longa Cooktown.'

When she demurred he mistook her meaning and agreed that perhaps the market place was hardly suitable and that it might be better to sell us privately. After all, he intimated, we lacked the lotus-skin and full moonface that in Chinese beauties brought such high prices. The Boss would probably make a better deal if he palmed us off quietly on some of his personal friends.

Ah Wong had only one possession – a set of small handleless pale-green tea cups, like the bowls of a doll's dinner service. One day, after he had been with us for some time, he invited us to his home in the cane cutters' quarters. Trembling with anticipation, we knocked at the door and were ushered into a room so neat that it might have come straight from a shop. It smelled deliriously of what we at first took to be pine-tar soap.

From a little cupboard Ah Wong took the fragile cups and set them carefully upon the floor. 'Chinese cups,' he explained proudly. 'Now, all-fellow dlink-im tea like in China.' He bowed low and with the gesture of one performing a ritual handed us each a cup. We sipped the thin green tea cautiously for fear of biting bits out of the edges.

There was a feeling of great peace in that room. Perhaps it came from the bareness of the place, or Ah Wong's ceremonious movements or the sweet foreign scent that filled the air. We breathed the room into us, tasting, smelling, absorbing. We gazed at the little beaded curtain that was rigged up in one corner. Before it, in an old jam jar, three scented sticks were burning. Watching the red ash creep down the green stems we were seized with curiosity.

'What's behind that curtain?' said somebody suddenly.

Ah Wong's eyelids came down like shutters over his eyes; his face was as expressionless as a closed door. We glanced questioningly at each other. What secret did the curtain hide? What possession? What image? Then, sudden as lightning, the truth struck home. Kate Clancy's phrase clicked into place in our minds. The heathen idol! At that moment we realised that Ah Wong was not a Christian.

Without a word to each other but as if at a signal, we rose, thanked him perfunctorily and hurried away. We needed to communicate our discovery and digest its implications. The excitement we had felt in drinking tea with Ah Wong faded beside the majestic news that his silence had made plain. For here was an opportunity such as is offered to few in this world, and we seized upon it greedily.

We were going to convert Ah Wong.

At this period we were immersed in those old stories wherein small children of extreme physical debility set so saintly an example that grown-up sinners were thereby brought to repentance. 'Misunderstood' was perhaps the best – or worst – of them.

It was unfortunate, of course, that none of us was in the least sickly. But we did not let that deter us. Luckily for the scheme, Ah Wong liked to be read to. His favourite story to date had been what he called 'The Siss Fambly Lobinson', particularly the part where the boa constrictor strangled the donkey. From this to the Book of Common Prayer was, we realised, a long jump, and we introduced it to him gradually. To our surprise, he was delighted with the new story. He loved to hear us intoning the responses and took pleasure in interjecting Amens.

The plan was working. In a short time he knew *Peep of Day*, our Bible primer, by heart.

'My word, Him bin pretty big-mob good fellow!' he would say appreciatively as the mighty story of the Gospels unrolled and he nodded over a favourite incident. Our hearts swelled. We decided to add hymns to the curriculum. It would never do for Ah Wong to be silent when, at the end of his mortal journey, St Peter handed him his harp. This move was particularly successful, and Ah Wong would top our shrill voices with his high tuneless singing that was like the cry of a sea bird.

Dere's a Flend for little childens
Above a blight, blue sky-ee ...

he would chant with relish. But his best efforts were reserved for

Hark, de helald angels singe-ee
Gloly to de newbone king-ee
Peace on earth and mercymile
Goddam sinners reconcile.

He sang this every day as he cooked the dinner.

At last the course seemed to us complete. Nothing remained but to take Ah Wong to church and get him christened. After the ceremony, our work done, we would decline and die, surrounded by proud and mournful relatives. It was a big price. But it was worth it.

Here, however, for the first time, we reckoned without Ah Wong. He had taken so kindly to the teaching that it was a shock to find he was not in the least interested in getting 'clissened'. In fact, quite definitely and mistrustfully against it.

'Me got jolly good-fellow Chinese name. What for me go to church, hey?'

We explained, patiently and with some reservations. We had not as yet revealed to Ah Wong that he was being turned into a Christian. Already we were aware that it is sometimes better not to tell the whole truth – at least, not all at once. It would be time enough for the disclosure when he had been baptised.

'Listen, Wong!' we said, and painted a festive picture of the joys of going to church. He would hear the organ, sing the hymns and kneel on a little red hassock. We told him about Mr Preston, the vicar, who would help him to get into Heaven. But Ah Wong was not impressed. He didn't want to go to church or to Heaven. He wanted to go to China. If he couldn't go to China he preferred to stay right here on the plantation. And who was 'Mister Pleston'? A big-mob good-fellow? One who would read him 'The Siss Fambly Lobinson'?

Well, we admitted, not that, exactly. But he would read the prayers beautifully.

Ah Wong snorted. He didn't *need* Mister Pleston. 'All you-fellow childens readee players jolly nice. Goodanuf for Ah Wong.'

This was an impasse. We were baulked. And angry. Ah Wong, we felt, had no right to come so far if he did not mean to go farther. Then somebody had an inspiration. As a crowning bait we told Ah Wong how, if he went to church, he would see our father, in his white silk suit with the crimson cummerbund, taking round the plate. This, to us, was a sight ever glorious. Sunday after Sunday we thrilled with pride as, singing the last hymn in a roaring baritone, Father took up the collection. Ah Wong, we added, would share with us the privilege of putting money into the plate.

But that, to our shocked surprise, was the last straw. Ah Wong shied away as though we had bitten him. What! Money on a plate! You put puddings on a plate, or lamb chops. But money—

'Whassa dam-silly-fellow nonsins?' he shouted wrathfully. 'Boss take-im money? I don't tink so. Boss all-along jolly fine fellow. Boss not take-im Ah Wong's money. And where I get-im money, hey? Ah Wong bin big-mob poor chap – no gotta no money!' But we knew better. Month after month Ah Wong added his new pay-cheque to the little package of cheques in the kitchen drawer. Again and again the Boss urged him to cash them but each time the shutter came down over Ah Wong's face as he shook his head.

'Me save-im,' he always said. He was polite, but final.

'But, Wong—' we protested, '*everybody* goes to church.'

It was no good. 'Church pretty silly stuff, I tink-im,' he said crossly. And that was the end. Our high hopes had come to nothing. As soon as he realised that *Peep of Day* and the hymns were stepping stones to church and not a new kind of entertainment, he resolutely put them aside. He even became suspicious of the 'Siss Fambly'. If the boa constrictor and the donkey had anything to do with being 'clissened' he was not going to have anything to do with *them*.

We were deeply conscious of failure. Yet we were aware, somehow, that it was not due wholly to our inadequacy. Dimly we realised that something else claimed Ah Wong, and that the symbol of its power was hidden behind his bead curtain where the sticks of incense burned. Thereafter we loved him with a deeper love for now it was mixed with sorrow and disappointment ...

If this story had no sequel it could properly end here. Indeed, we thought it had ended when a year or so later we said goodbye to Ah Wong. The Boss had died suddenly and we were going south with our mother to a life which would never again include plantations and Chinese cooks.

Ah Wong stood on the murky station platform waiting for the train to move. The black eyes gazed broodingly in through the window upon the family he had tended. Nothing was said for a long while. It is difficult to speak when there is too much to say.

The guard waved his green light. Ah Wong put his fingers in our mother's black-gloved hand. In them he held a small red calico poppy.

'Belonga flower-hat,' he explained. 'I find-im. Maybe Missus put on flower-hat again some day-ee!'

Her mouth trembled as they gazed at each other. She took the poppy and the whistle blew. 'Goodby-ee!' he said shrilly. 'Be good, all-fellow childens!'

'Don't forget to cash your cheques, Wong!' we cried, waving wildly. He smiled and shook his head.

'I save-im,' we heard him say as the train steamed out . . .

That, we thought, was the end of him. And so it was, for the rest of the family. But I, through luck, chance, coincidence, was to see Ah Wong once more.

Some years later I was taken on the staff of a well-known Australian newspaper. The youngest cub reporter was detailed to take me on his assignments and teach me the trade. He was nineteen and, to my eyes, a man of considerable experience and learning. When the editor handed me over he regarded me gloomily and with marked distaste.

'What am I to do with it?' he enquired bitterly. 'Wheel it around in a perambulator?'

Outside the office he made it clear that I was to be his slave. And in that capacity I trudged after him from assignment to assignment, rejoicing in any crumb from his journalistic table.

He met me one day, looking as though he had just been done out of a legacy. 'Listen, kid! We're up the spout,' he said gloomily. 'We've got to interview a fellow who can only talk French. And I don't know a word of the beastly lingo.'

As humbly as possible and secretly blessing the names of departed Mademoiselles, I intimated that I could speak French.

'Only a little—' I added hurriedly, so as not to offend him. He looked at me disbelievingly. It seemed to him hardly possible. A cub reporter's cub reporter!

'All right,' he said finally, his face clearing. 'You do it and I'll sign it. Here's the address.' And he strode off leaving a slip of paper in my hand.

'Sailing ship *Santa Lucia*, coming from Lima, calling at all eastern Australian ports,' I read. 'Interview Third Officer Alexis Bronowsky. Russian, but speaks French. Get a story on his cargo.'

My heart thumped. Here was I, on my first assignment. My own name was shouting to me from all the books that eventually would result from it. And there was the *Santa Lucia*, a grimy, battered ship crouching against the wharf, her furled sails grey with wind and water. But I saw, as I came up the gangway, that her decks were white and every strip of metal twinkled in the sun.

The third officer had a slow, lounging sailor's walk. He was very young and his manner, as he led me round the ship, suggested that the whole of time was at our disposal. He insisted on having every landmark in Sydney Harbour pointed out to him. Indeed, it seemed as though he and not I were doing the interviewing. He spoke at length of his own career which seemed to me, as to himself, thoroughly glorious. Only after that did I get a chance to remind him about the cargo.

Nom de Dieu! He had entirely forgotten it! '*Allons!*' he said and led me down ladder after ladder until we seemed to be in the hold of the ship. Standing beside a door, he paused and beckoned.

'It will be very dark,' he whispered warningly. 'They are so old. They do not like the light.'

'Who are so old?' I whispered back.

'The cargo. The old men. They are going back to China to die. All their lives they have saved their money so that they may have enough to take them home. You will see.'

Then, very quietly, he opened the door. Out of the darkness there rose a strong, musty human smell mixed with incense. As my eyes grew accustomed to the gloom I saw that the hold was filled with layer on layer of narrow bunks. And in each, passive and inert, lay an old man. Occasionally one opened his eyes and looked at us without curiosity. Grey pigtails swung limply from the bunks, wrinkled hands and feet hung over the sides seeking a little coolness in the hot, sleepy air. The imminence of death was everywhere but to my own surprise the scene had no horror for me. Life had come full circle in the hold of the *Santa Lucia*. The old men in their youth had scattered to the points of the earth. Now they were going home to die.

The third officer touched my arm. 'Come!' he whispered, and drew me gently away from the door.

At that moment a thin voice spoke from a bunk beneath me. 'Big-fellow Little Missy!' it said softly.

Oh, that familiar phrase! It came straight out of the past, dissolving me into my earliest elements. The green fronds of cane were about me, the smells of the hold mingled with the scent of incense in Ah Wong's room on the plantation. I turned and scrambled down the ladder.

'Where are you, Wong?' I whispered. And then I saw him.

He was lying in one of the lower bunks, his pig-tail dangling to the floor. His black eyes stared from his face. He was just the same – frailer, of course, a shrunken image of the old Ah Wong, but the same in essence. He smiled at me and I took his hands in mine as we gazed at each other. Once again there was nothing to be said because there was too much to say.

'Did you cash your cheques, Wong?' I whispered at last.

He raised himself slightly and nodded. 'I cashim, Missy. I all-along save-im, buy-im boat tickee. Now Ah Wong go home.'

He slipped down to his bunk again and closed his eyes. Even so slight a contact with life was already too much for him. Very gently I pulled the blanket over his hands.

'Tell Missus Ah Wong all-time tink-im velly kind thoughts.'

'I'll do that. Goodbye, now, Wong!'

'Goodby-ee now, Missy. Be all-along good-fellow child!' he said faintly and turned his head away.

I stumbled after the third officer up the companionways into the sunlight. The sudden glare was dazzling. I was unsteady with tears and memory and the sight of dying men. Silently I prayed that he would not ask me to explain.

But he asked nothing. Merely smiled at me. '*N'expliquez-pas!*' he said gently and turned me towards the gangway.

Happiness filled me. Running for the tram I was flooded with a tide of life all the richer for coming straight from death. Infinite with experience, the world opened before me, itself borne upon that living stream. And I knew that Ah Wong was flooded with it, too. Like all those who are very young I had made the mistake of thinking that there were separate rivers of life and death. Now I knew that there is only one tide, whole and indivisible. The same flood that was flinging me into life was taking Ah Wong home ...

The Santa Lucia

Johnny Delaney

To
Frieda Heidecke Stern
for showing me the way through the Canyon

Wenn ein Tuer ʒue geht
an anders Tuerle geht uff.

Whenever I think of him I am carried down into the wells of childhood. The deepest memories of men, as of birds, are contained within the nest; and down there, at the bottom of the well, lies the figure of Johnny Delaney – a little grain of truth for me – sending up his endless message to the surface of the water. I often wonder how that melodious Irish name came to be borne across the seas to our sprawling plantation in the tropics of Australia. For it is there that we must look for him, not in his native land. I cannot remember the cane-fields without remembering Johnny. And at this moment he is so close, I could almost touch his hand. Or his black, Irish head, perhaps. Or his little thin bow-legs.

I suppose you would have said that he was primarily a jockey. That, at any rate, was the form of address he preferred. But he was also groom, stable-boy and carpenter; even, when labour was short, a cane cutter, and sometimes a feeder at the mill. It seems to me now that there was nothing Johnny could not do, no part of our family life in which he was not the dominating figure. Before any of the children came he was already part of the plantation – like the house itself, and the black-fellows, and the groves of mango trees. Indeed, when we were very young, we thought we had three parents – not only our father and mother but Johnny Delaney as well. As soon as a child began to stagger, he snatched it away from sheltering arms as though, like the warlocks in fairy tales, he had come to claim his own. The moment it was strong enough to wave a rattle he taught it to handle reins, and in no time he had it climbing palm trees to strengthen its riding muscles. Long before it could properly talk it was

shown the difference between poisonous snakes and the ones that have no sting; the proper method of avoiding tarantulas; how to make grown-up life a torture with whistles from bamboo sticks; and to hide from Kate Clancy, our gorgon nurse, in the stems of the sugar-cane. And there, in that last phrase, lies the clue to Johnny Delaney. He was, before anything else, an antisocial being. He was a man made entirely of blackness and shadow, the quickest-tempered, arrogantest, bitter-heartedest creature that ever stepped out of the County Clare. But the whole family loved him with a deep and changeless passion. Don't ask me why. Just let me tell you Johnny's story, and I think you will not wonder.

He had two gifts – if gift is a proper word to use in connection with so determined a have-not as Johnny. He could swear. He could swear in a way that would blister the skin of a camel. Not like a trooper, profanely. Johnny Delaney was an artist and that would have been beneath him. No. His swearing was like a bitter poem, a long, black, vitriolic epic, invented by himself. Dark words and phrases flowed from his lips in cascades and fountains of rage. And once at it, he could hold an audience shocked and stunned for half an hour together.

'And take *that* into yer gizzards!' he would conclude venomously, as his hearers stumbled away.

The smallest thing was enough to set him going and once you had heard the first phrase it was impossible not to listen to the end, the invention was so superb. The mere sight of a priest enraged him; and he deliberately pressed his hat a little further on his head when he met Mr Preston, the vicar. The gesture was sufficiently obvious; no one could mistake his meaning. 'Ah, what do they know of life at all, them ignorant white angels? Sittin' an' sthrummin' their harps of gold with never a shadow upon them!' If he had known that Father Connolly and Mr Preston would both officiate at his grave – for they, too, recognised his essence – I don't believe he'd have died. He'd have gone on living till Judgement Day, simply out of spite.

His other gift was second sight. Oh, not Cassandra's splendid vision nor her high sense of tragedy. Johnny Delaney's premonitions were essentially domestic. I remember watching my father once, shading his eyes with his big grass hat, as he scanned the horizon anxiously. For my mother was out by herself in the dog-cart, driving a newly broken mare. Johnny, about as high as his elbow, stood by with his lips pursed sourly. 'Sure, the Misthress is safe as a nail in a post,' he was saying with bitter conviction. 'Isn't it, now, a wastheful thing, a woman to be sitting as live as a bee and a good horse dead in the ditch?' His fore-warning was exactly true. They found the dog-cart overturned, the mare with both her hind legs broken and my mother sitting by the side of the road with the dying head in her lap.

When Johnny heard that a third baby was expected he gave a loud and prolonged groan. 'Another girl!' he said lugubriously. 'Two years till we get a bhoy!' And no one was at all surprised when he proved to be quite right.

On another occasion, when an urgent telegram arrived, he remarked gleefully – and correctly – to my mother – 'It'll be that ould divil, yer father's brother, dhropped dead at the Counthry Show.

Well, our lives'll all be brighther without him, if he hasn't embezzled yer trust funds.'

Contrariwise – and Johnny Delaney was always contrary – he never attempted to use his gift to foretell the result of a race. Racing was to him, as to my father, a sacred occupation. He was quick, however, to pocket a bribe when asked to name a winner. Then – sardonically watching the hopeful smile spread over the questioner's face – he would whisper in the eager ear, 'The besth horse, surely!' All things considered, it is quite surprising that Johnny was never knifed.

Nor would he consult his inward crystal to forward his own affairs. No man living can have cared less about the future. All he ever said in regard to it was, 'I'll die the day me work is done and not a minyut before.' The grown-ups took this for just another piece of arrogance. But we, steeped in myth and fairy tale, understood it differently. It was perfectly obvious to us that Johnny was immortal and, furthermore, that he knew it.

That this should be so did not surprise us. Of course he would live till the end of time, for when – with horses and sugar-cane – is anyone's work ever finished? Only when the last horse is dead and sugar ceases to grow. Not until we grew older did we realise that Johnny had another work besides his daily chores.

Johnny's person, you would have said, was a perfect match for his tongue. An ugly, long-toothed face he had, criss-crossed like the map of Mars. From a narrow head his ears stuck out like two enormous handles. His spirit glared through his dark eyes, a fierce, tormented prisoner. And his mouth had a wry and bitter twist that was seldom smoothed out by a smile. From behind, however, and at a distance – particularly when he was dressed in his racing colours – he looked like an elegant little boy. That, indeed, is how many a stranger saw him. He only needed to turn his head to correct the delightful illusion.

None of us, not even our father, who had known

him intimately for many years, knew Johnny Delaney's secret – what pain, what passion or despair, had worked upon his spirit. A modern psychologist or a conventional mind might have looked to his hump for the cause. But they would have been wrong. Johnny's hump was his treasure. 'It's me house, it's me parlour!' he would tell us arrogantly, glancing with pity at our flat, skinny shoulders. 'I'm a snail with me palace on me back, and it's there I rethire when I wish to take me ease.' Whenever he shut the door of his room we imagined Johnny – like a snail – drawing his black head into the hump and taking his ease within it. A lordly relaxation.

Johnny's was the only hut in the compound whose inside we did not know. Matt Heffernan's – the overseer – was untidy, dirty and smelly. Pictures of well-fed naked ladies smiled softly from the walls. The room of Ah Wong, the Chinese cook, had nothing in it at all. Except for the mat on which he slept it was clean and empty as the husk of a nut. Only Johnny barred us out, berating us malevolently if we put a toe on his threshold. His hut, like his hump, was his palace. None but the master could take their ease within.

'But what do you do in there, Johnny?' we would ask him inquisitively.

'Me life's work,' he would reply sharply, and shut his mouth like a trap.

Outside his hut, however, he had no sense of personal property. He behaved towards the world with a grandiose, contemptuous air – as though he had originally created it and had now no further use for his handiwork. Money meant nothing to him. Sometimes he would 'blow' a pay-cheque on a drinking bout in MacKinley, where the friendly jailer locked him up until he was sober again. But apart from these rare occasions he gave his earnings away casually, as though they were bits of paper. Nevertheless – contemptuous though he was of his own riches – he watched our open-handed father with the eye of an anxious eagle.

'Go on, then, give it to him!' he would jeer, as the hand reached quickly into the pocket in response to a hard-luck story. 'The Misthress, dear soul, can take in washin' and yez can put the childer to scarin' rooks from Misther Preston's cane.' Only when Johnny's back was turned could my father nip into the Kingdom of Heaven by warming a palm with silver.

But if Johnny was generous with his riches, he was a prince, a sheikh, a Grand Caliph when it came to giving advice. Nobody was free from it; everyone suffered equally. He told Kate Clancy to buy rouge from the chemist instead of 'robbin' the Masther's purse' by using the cochineal. 'Yer face is a disasther now. Would yez want it to be a ruin?' Matt Heffernan, always in trouble with the local belles, was driven to the edge of madness by Johnny's advice on the subject. 'Ah, leave them! Be a hermit, Matt. Don't insult the mighty realm of nature by mating with schraps of tinsel!'

Ah Wong, on the other hand, seemed to welcome his diatribes. 'Yess, Johnee! No, Johnee! I tink-im plurry good words,' he would say, nodding his head solemnly. The smooth Eastern face absorbed all jibes and irony. It smiled and kept its thoughts to itself. Nothing disturbed that pool of wisdom. And I think Johnny found a moment's peace as his barbs went home to silence.

He hectored our father's friends and guests on their habits, professions and private lives; and never failed, after their first fury, to draw forth sheepish grins of agreement. Once a grown-up cousin, lamenting an unfortunate love-affair, took a trip to the plantation for the sole purpose of consulting Johnny. With her city muslins sweeping the dust, she sat on the edge of an upturned feed-bucket – an exquisite, eager Niobe – weeping out her woes to him while he curry-combed the horses. We heard nothing of what passed between them. Indeed, I think it probable that Johnny never uttered a word. But he let out a banshee wail of mirth over and over again – hollow and wild and inhuman. Evidently it solved something. For she came back dry-eyed from the stables walking with a light gay step and a look of peace on her face.

But such outside advice was intermittent. To the family it came as a steady downpour. He advised our father about his investments and our mother about her hats. 'If it only had a melon, now, the thing would be complete!' That was his comment on a flowery concoction that my mother never wore again for fear of arousing his wrath.

But these things were trifles. Johnny Delaney's prime concern was to teach our parents how to bring up their children. 'Root, shoot and fruit' must be eaten every day. Ipecacuanha wine was the cure for all ailments. Nightlights had to burn in the nursery to keep away 'things and witches'. A naughty child must never be spanked but 'straightway sent to Coventry'. It was his strong – and quite correct – conviction that for anyone not to be spoken to was the worst of all shames.

On the other hand, there were many times when he would not let *us* speak. Emotional times, cowardly times, times of personal trouble. I remember standing on the shaky bridge that crossed our little creek. The planks were hot beneath my feet and the rail burned in my hand. The brown water rushed away in a thick curdle below me. Out of nowhere – for I was a thoughtless child – I was struck by the awful realisation that merely to be alive, to live, was a matter of great courage. And that all men in their secret selves were somehow innocent victims; the wounded in no worse a case than the wounder and both of them betrayed. I say awful realisation – for if it was true I would have to do something about it. My past, such as it was, was over. From now on I could never live according to like and dislike. I should have to take people as *they* were, accept and not judge. A desperate, frightening notion.

I tried, abashed and stammering, to communicate these thoughts to Johnny. But he stopped me at once. 'Ah, whisht then!' he said angrily. 'That's no sort of thought for the young. Let yez get a skin like the armadillo and hathred rise in yer bhreast like yeast!' (When hatred comes it brings great peace. A bright flower lifts its head within us. But what if the flower cannot rise? What if its head is for ever bowed by the painful rain of justice and love?) Johnny looked at me with furious eyes. But I knew, in that moment of clarity, that he wasn't talking to me. He was warning *himself* against 'all such thruck'; giving himself the stern injunction he never could truly obey. Armadillo skins are not for all. There are some that must go uncovered.

Johnny had no favourites. If he loved one of us more than another nobody would have guessed it. And he knew our natures through and through as though they were lessons he'd learned.

'This wan must be yer care,' he said once,

morosely nodding at the eldest child. 'Yez must watch her keenly when I'm gone.'

But our mother had her eye on her darling, the beautiful second sister. 'But surely, Johnny,' she protested, 'it's *she* we must watch!' For her mind was busy with strings of suitors, all eager to snatch her jewel.

Johnny eyed her viciously. '*She's* safe. She has her nose in herself. But this wan's black with loving!'

Black with loving. Curious phrase. Our parents shook uncomprehending heads and left it hanging in the air, another of Johnny's mysteries. Had they argued they would have said conventionally that love is always bright. Johnny knew better. He saw the child in her coils of passion and knew she was lost from the start. The lover is always dark and naked. His share is shadow and the point of the sword. The blood moves slowly through his heart; it flows very thick and black. He goes with one hand shielding his eyes and the other imploringly flung outwards. The loved can sit in the lap of time and play with their toys and sleep. The lover has to watch and pray. He is involved with the nature of things, simply by being a lover. He has to grind his own grain; no other bread will feed him. It is he, going forward against the thorn, who needs to be treasured and cared for; the loved are always safe.

I think, too, that Johnny, when he used that phrase, was telling us unconsciously the story of himself. If ever there was a man, dark and cloudy and black with loving, it was little Johnny Delaney. It burned within him secretly in some Pluto cavern of being. That central glowing seam of coal ravaged his outward substance. He and the earth were brother and sister, seared and scored on their visible surface, because of the pits at the heart. But on earth there are men with pick and shovel to set that dark mass free. They mine it to glow on human hearthstones and redeem itself in flame. For Johnny there were no such mediators. His bitter tongue could not say the words, nor his seared face give evidence. His love was heavy and silent within him. Not even the children could make it speak.

But what, after all, do words matter? Once they are uttered they are lost – to the hearer as well as the speaker. And the angel comes by silently and takes us all with a sigh. We *knew* Johnny. And it is a truism that the race of children has little need of words. He was mixed with our inmost hearts and spirits. He belonged to us far more nearly than ever our parents could. Their love was our rightful privilege. We were no more grateful to them for it than for sunshine or air. But Johnny was an extra thing, a special dispensation. He lifted our lives from their dull round into a kind of legend. All pasts, good and bad, are like a story. Whenever we try to return to them we see ourselves as fairy-tale figures, slightly larger than life. If I were to go back now to the plantation I know I would walk with the step of a prince because of Johnny Delaney. And the country round about the cane-

Johnny Delaney

fields would reek with his lordly myths.

The flamingo-swamp – how well I remember! – was one of his favourite landmarks. For there it was that Boydie McGrew was buried alive by a bushranger. At night his ghost went wildly crying across the watery wasteland – 'Take me out of the bog, bhoys, take me out of the bog!' 'I can hear him wailing,' Johnny would say, 'like the voice of me own brother!' Down at the place where the creek forked we would seize each other's hands – none of us ever dared to take Johnny's – for there, full of drink and evil years, old Paddy Freeman was drowned. 'And, faith, his body's down there still, as tight as the dhrum in a band!' He would stand by the gunyahs in the bush, moodily watching the black-fellows and their flocks of mongrel dogs. He'd a friend among them, Billy Pee-kow, one of the cane cutters. Johnny never failed to give him advice on how to dance a corroboree or to pitch a boomerang. But afterwards he would turn away and fall into sombre brooding. 'A vanishing race,' he would say with a sigh, while we waited expectantly. We would not have been in the least surprised if the smiling blacks and their shy women had dis-solved before our eyes.

But of all the fearful, exciting land-marks, the place by the pond where the snake bit Johnny was the worst – or rather, the best. 'Snake is it?' he would say, jeering, when asked to repeat the story. 'A serpent it was, from the Garden of Eden, and few men last out that!' We thrilled with pride and reflected glory. Any man could be bitten by a snake but only the tempter out of Eden would do for Johnny Delaney. 'Not Adam and Eve's serpent, surely, Johnny?' 'The same!' he would cry with triumphant malice, and we shiv-ered together with horrid joy at getting so near to the Bible. We might have been walking with Cain himself, through the green Australian bush.

And always, no matter where we went, Johnny's dark eyes would be gravely searching, in the undergrowth and scrub. Birds' nests, lizards or what, we wondered? Suddenly he would dart from the path and seize a little fallen branch or a gnarled piece of wood. Every time he wandered into the bush he brought home two or three of these treasures. His thick, knotty fingers handled them delicately; he would smooth and roll them between his palms and test their hardness with the blade of his knife. And to every question as to why he wanted them he made the same reply. 'It's me life's work,' he would say darkly with a look that closed the subject. The curiosity this aroused was almost unbearable. The riddle of the Sphinx – had we heard of it – would have seemed a very minor thing compared with Johnny's work. Was he building a little house, perhaps? Did he burn the wood at dead of night beneath some warlock's brew? Or was he – surely nothing so dull! – simply a collector? But Johnny Delaney kept his secret. We did not discover the nature of his work until his work was done.

Johnny's first concern with regard to us was to give us education. He had very definite ideas on the proper accomplishments for the young. One was Knot-tying. We could all have vied with any sailor at a very early age. Another was Spitting. Not merely ejecting saliva but spitting as an art. He taught us the Long Spit and the Drop Spit and, last, the Over the Shoulder. In this, as in all else, he was a perfectionist. He roared, swore and jibed at us until, from sheer weariness, we became good enough to pass. From the earnest attention he gave this pastime you would have thought that our future lives were all to be spent in bar-rooms full of trickily placed spittoons. To this day I cannot see a man spitting in the street without a feeling of contempt for his lack of aplomb, vulgar disregard of artistry, and ignorance of proper targets and the way to aim at them.

There were, however, genteeler aspects to Johnny's compulsory training. These were 'Singin', Community Dancin' and a Thorough Knowledge of the Stars and Constellations'. In the latter subject we never got further than Orion's Belt, the Southern Cross and Berenice's Hair. Possibly because Johnny's own grasp of the stars was limited and chancy. We could jig, however, and dance a reel like any Aran Islander. And in the matter of singing, though his voice was as harsh as a mountain hawk's, Johnny was no mean tutor. That man could have made the angels sing, simply by swearing at them. Almost before we could say the words, he had us on firsts and seconds. Glowering, he would stand before us, conducting with a stick of cane, while 'Believe me if all' and 'Rendal, my son' streeled thinly from our lips. But above all other songs, he preferred our two-part rendering of that melancholy chant—

She's the most disthressful cou-un-three
That iver yet was seen—
They're hangin' men an' women for
The Wearin' o' the Green

When Matt Heffernan, to get some of his own back, secretly taught us 'The Battle of the Boyne' – that song so loved of Orangemen – Johnny gave one of his best performances. The swearing lasted for forty-five minutes. For Johnny, as you will have guessed, was politically a Rebel.

In addition to tutoring us on the plantation, Johnny constituted himself our guardian on the rare occasions when we left it. Among our father's idiosyncrasies was a mania for collecting every possible sort of conveyance. A four-wheeler, a hansom cab, an old howdah and an elegant sledge were housed together in the barn with carts, wagons and sulkies. Whether he hoped he would someday have a paved road for the four-wheeler, an elephant for the howdah and a fall of snow for the crimson sledge nobody ever knew. The only one of the four oddities that could be used in the bush was the hansom. And in this we were driven to the town of MacKinley for clothes, dentist and parties. There we would sit in the hot little box, with cane and paw-paw, mango and orange brushing greenly by the windows. Behind, high up in the driving seat, sat Johnny with his whip. Through the opening in the roof his face would peer down from time to time, looking like a mouldy patch on the ceiling. At the end of the drive he would stumble down, swing back the doors with a princely gesture, and tweak us out one by one. If we were going to the dentist he would murmur banefully 'Exthractions!' If to a party, he would sweep us with a disgusted glance, wet the corner of his handkerchief on our tongues and give a last rub to our faces. Once, after somebody's birthday dance, the youngest child salvaged a chocolate cat to take home to our mother. As soon as he saw it Johnny snatched it away and proceeded to lick its melting contours into a shape more feline. 'And who's to tell her?' he demanded when one of us dared to protest. 'Ye'd insult the woman giving her a lump the like o' that!'

I shall always remember MacKinley – that ugly little wooden town with its corrugated roofs. Not only because of our trips with Johnny but because it was in MacKinley that we last saw Johnny alive. Maybe he was older than we guessed. Or perhaps the friction of his inward nature had worn his life away. Death and Johnny – it seems to me now – were never far apart. For a long time – even the children could see it – he had been growing thinner. Then he suddenly developed a cough so cavernous that his bones seemed to rattle with it. In vain our parents pleaded with him, to rest, to take a vacation. He only answered them viciously and worked with doubled zest. Demons of speed and work were in him. His advice grew more malevolent daily and his swearing more inventive. He seemed to have reached his inmost seam of bane and tribulation.

When he was not in the stables, or presiding over family affairs, he was darting about the ripened cane-fields jeering the cutters on. And at evening when we passed his room we would hear him muttering to himself as he sat within his hump.

Then one day, after the cane was cut, he galloped into MacKinley. We heard later that his last three pay-cheques were in his pocket and that he had 'blown' them gloriously. When at night the policeman, out of pure friendship, popped him into the lock-up there wasn't a man in the whole township who hadn't been treated by Johnny.

I remember our father's look of concern when somebody told him the news. 'That'll finish him!' he said angrily. And the next thing we knew we were in the dog-cart, driving through the shadowy bush instead of going to bed. It was a lucky thing for us that Kate was staying away with her brother. We should never have been allowed otherwise to embark on such an adventure.

The excitement of sleeping in MacKinley's hotel

was doubled for us by Johnny's coughing. It reached us from the rackety lock-up that stood a few yards away; and our dreams that night were punctuated by the hollow, mournful sound. In the morning, before anyone else was awake, we crept out through the beer-smelling bar and stood beneath the lock-up windows in fearful expectation. There, within the walls, was Johnny. Invisible to our watching eyes but terrifyingly audible. It was like being in some dreadful story, to stand outside in the burning sun and listen to that cough. Clamped to the door was a big black lock. There were thick black irons at the window. We were stifled and choked, as if we were drowning. Johnny to be shut away in there and we not able to see him! A panic ran through all of us; we stared at each other in terror. But suddenly – as though at a whispered, secret order – the air flowed back again to our lungs and we all began to sing. The tune came thin and shaky at first, because of our dreadful excitement.

Believe me if all those endearing young charms
That I gaze on so fondly today—

And, as if by magic, at the first phrase, a face appeared at the window. One bar flung a shadow across his brow, and between two others came Johnny's hand, beating time with a tin teaspoon. Cocking his head to one side – an old familiar gesture – he listened to our rising voices for a hint of a flat note. He waved the teaspoon peremptorily and between his coughs he nodded sternly, drawing the altos and tenors from us with never a smile of praise. From his expression he might have been conducting the Bach Choir or a group of backward angels. We sang on, right through the repertoire, with Johnny naming each song in turn and the town of MacKinley gathering behind us, gaping up at the window.

'Now, "You'll tak the high-road"!' commanded Johnny, as we came to the end of 'Rendal'. But at that moment – why at *that* moment? – the awful cruelty of childhood rose into all our breasts. As Johnny waited expectantly, holding his teaspoon high, we swung into Heffernan's 'Battle' song with a tuneless, taunting shriek—

O-o-o oh, we're up to our necks in Irish blood,
We're up to our necks in slaughter!

Were we not safe, out here in the sun? Wasn't Johnny up there behind the bars and a big black lock on the door? There was nothing he could do to us and everything we could do to him.

And didn't we give the Irish Hell
At the Battle of Boiling Water?

In desperate and painful elation we came to the end of the ugly song and waited for the storm. But there was silence. No sound but the clink of metal on stone as the teaspoon fell to the ground. Johnny clasped the bars with his knotty fingers and leaned

his head on his hands. Defeat and resignation were in that gesture – as though he had received, and accepted, a painful mortal wound. Then he raised his head. His face had a sweet and terrible sadness as he gazed down upon us. Locked there like an ape, a trapped wild creature, he looked at us through the bars. Then he said, in a soft, beseeching whisper – 'Childer, little childer, do yez want to break me heart?'

There was such gentleness, such awful mildness in those words, that we were lost and abandoned. We did not know what to do nor where to go. A dreadful sense of shame filled us; we dared not look at him. But we flung ourselves, repentant and loving, against the wall of the lock-up.

'Johnny! Johnny! Johnny!' we cried, as though by repeating the beloved name we would somehow be forgiven. And we were forgiven – in Johnny's peculiar way.

A familiar stream of imprecation came pouring down from the window. Johnny's face, as it glared

out through the bars, was now a cauldron of rage.
We stood beneath the fountain of fury absolved by
the pelting words. The sad, beseeching gentleness
had thrust us into the cold. Now we were home and
warm again, saved by the flood of his anger. Behind
us the township murmured proudly. 'He's at the
top of his form today; I never heard him better!'

'And take that into yer wretched gizzards!' came
Johnny's peroration. Then the raging face disap-
peared from the window; nothing was heard from
within the lock-up but a paroxysm of coughing . . .

It was days before we saw Johnny again and by
that time he was beyond the power of man or child
to hurt him.

From the lock-up he was taken to the hospital
and only released from that second prison
because he insisted to our father that he must
come home 'for a while or two' to finish his life's
work.

They brought him back in an ambulance, two

nights before Christmas. And they left him alone, in his old hut, at his own angry insistence. In the morning they found him dead. It had only taken a few hours to do what he had to do.

'Johnny's gone to Heaven,' said our mother, with a sort of tearful brightness.

We looked at her disbelievingly. Johnny had despised Heaven. To have gone there would have been clear against his principles. Johnny Delaney a blackleg? We thought it extremely unlikely. Unless, of course, God needed him to teach the angels to spit.

'I suppose you mean he's dead,' said somebody, and our mother, seeing her careful myth dissolve, simply wept and said yes.

'Well, now we can have his emu's egg,' said another child calmly.

'Oh, heartless, heartless!' cried our mother, looking at us in terror; seeing, perhaps, her own death and the four of us wrangling over her jewels.

But we were not heartless. We were using a common childish device to protect ourselves from disaster. Children have strong and deep emotions but no mechanism to deal with them. If once they let their hearts fill up they know that they will be drowned. So they seize on the nearest objective thing to keep down the rising flood. Our amulet was the emu's egg, twofold in healing magic. For it held within it Johnny's death and at the same time brought us safely past it.

Before he was buried they took us to see him. The incongruity of Johnny being in two places at once – Heaven and his own bed – did not occur to our parents. They never thought of hiding him from us. In those days death was not a shocking affair that should not be shown to children. You lived, you loved, you gave birth and you died and none of these dynamic functions was separable from the others.

I remember feeling no fear when I saw him. Death gives a great upsurge of strength and sweetened life to the living. Like a stone at the bottom of a well he lay, with the room swinging round in widening rings away and away to the surface. Only his feet disturbed me. They were not lying flat with the rest of his body, which seemed to be flush with the bed. They were tipped up sharply, forward marching, as though they had already set out on a walk that led through the ceiling. I looked away from them hurriedly and kept my eyes on his face. My chief thought, as I gazed at him, was that white was somehow wrong for Johnny – he was always so very black. He looked absurdly quiet and silent, except for that sardonic smile that made him seem our familiar friend, even in his shroud. It cheered me – that smile. I thought he had left it behind for us as a sort of legacy. But apart from the smile, it seemed to me, his body hardly mattered at all. I was far more interested, like the rest of the children, in searching Johnny's room. We stared round eagerly.

The hut was impersonal and tidy; it smelt of dust and gumleaves. In one corner hung his jockey-cap and the cerise blouse with the blue armbands, and the white pants and his whip. Below them on the chest of drawers, the emu's egg shone brightly. On the wall hung a faded newspaper picture of our mother bending her doe-like face over her first baby. But these were not the things we sought. Where was his life's work, we wanted to know. What had he done with the wood?

'Look!' said our father quietly, his feet like thunder on the wooden floor as he tiptoed away from the bed.

Then we turned to the little carpenter's bench and saw the group of figures. There were carved and painted kings and children kneeling beside a stable. No shepherds with flocks of snowy lambs, no angels with folded wings. Instead there were little native creatures – kangaroos, emus, red flamingos; horses and lizards and goats. The kneeling men were cane cutters, offering green cane boughs; swagmen with blankets rolled on their shoulders; drovers carrying whips in their hands and their steers standing meekly by. The crowned figures were rough likenesses of our father, Ah Wong and Billy Pee-kow. The four children in blue smocks – recognisably ourselves – knelt down at the edge of the stable. And alone – apart from men and beasts – stood a little bowed hump-backed figure, with a jockey-cap in its hand. It seemed to be gazing at the crib, which was padded with yellow strips of straw from the sheath of a champagne bottle. The Child lay in it, rosy and gay, waving His hand at the scene. All that was lacking was His halo, which was clutched in Johnny Delaney's hand when they found him dead in the morning.

It was lying now, a golden ring, beside a red flamingo. Our mother leaned across our heads and lifted it from the bench.

'This must go with him,' she said gently, 'the last thing he touched.'

'No,' said the eldest child, with a smile. 'He doesn't want it now.'

She took the little golden ring and, lifting the Child from the rough crib, she set it on His head. It clicked home neatly, firm and sure, and Johnny Delaney's life work was complete.

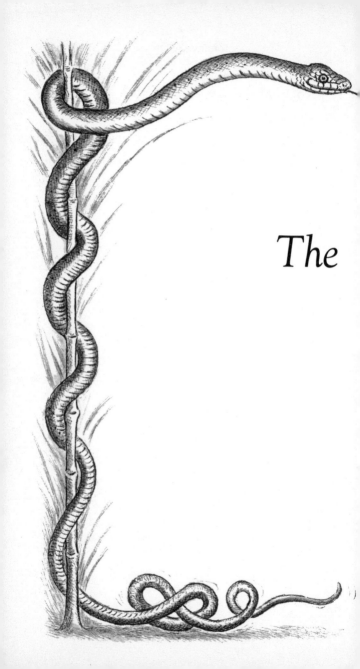

The

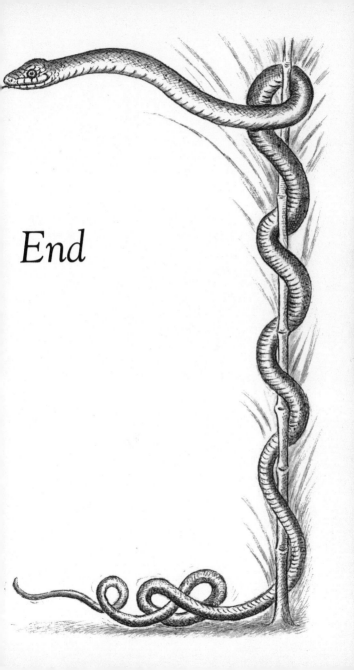

End

P. L. Travers was born Helen Lyndon Goff in 1899 in Queensland, Australia. She worked as a dancer and an actress, but writing was her real love and she turned to journalism. Travers set sail for England in 1924 and became an essayist, theatre and film critic, and scholar of folklore and myth. While recuperating from a serious illness Travers wrote *Mary Poppins* – 'to while away the days, but also to put down something that had been in my mind for a long time,' she said. It was first published in 1934 and was an instant success. *Mary Poppins* has gone on to become one of the best-loved classics in children's literature and has enchanted generations. In addition to the *Mary Poppins* books, Travers wrote novels, poetry and non-fiction. She received an OBE in 1977 and died in 1996.